Cuba, Old and New

by

Albert Gardner Robinson

The Echo Library 2007

Published by

The Echo Library

Echo Library
131 High St.
Teddington
Middlesex TW11 8HH

www.echo-library.com

Please report serious faults in the text to complaints@echo-library.com

ISBN 978-1-40683-950-0

CONTENTS

CHAPTER
- I. OLD CUBA
- II. NEW CUBA
- III. THE COUNTRY
- IV. THE OLD HAVANA
- V. THE NEW HAVANA
- VI. AROUND THE ISLAND
- VII. AROUND THE ISLAND (*Continued*)
- VIII. THE UNITED STATES AND CUBA
- IX. CUBA'S REVOLUTIONS
- X. INDEPENDENCE
- XI. FILIBUSTERING
- XII. THE STORY OF SUGAR
- XIII. VARIOUS PRODUCTS AND INDUSTRIES
- XIV. POLITICS, GOVERNMENT, AND COMMERCE

I

OLD CUBA

Christopher Columbus was a man of lively imagination. Had he been an ordinary, prosaic and plodding individual, he would have stayed at home combing wool as did his prosaic and plodding ancestors for several generations. At the age of fourteen he went to sea and soon developed an active curiosity about regions then unknown but believed to exist. There was even then some knowledge of western Asia, and even of China as approached from the west. Two and two being properly put together, the result was a reasonable argument that China and India could be reached from the other direction, that is, by going westward instead of eastward.

In the early autumn of the year 1492, Columbus was busy discovering islands in the Caribbean Sea region, and, incidentally, seeking for the richest of the group. From dwellers on other islands, he heard of one, called Cubanacan, larger and richer than any that he had then discovered. A mixture of those tales with his own vivid imagination produced a belief in a country of wide extent, vastly rich in gold and gems, and already a centre of an extensive commerce. Cruising in search of what he believed to be the eastern coast of Asia, he sighted the shore of Cuba on the morning of October 28, 1492. His journal, under date of October 24, states: "At midnight I tripped my anchors off this *Cabo del Isleo de Isabella*, where I was pitched to go to the island of Cuba, which I learn from these people is very large and magnificent, and there are gold and spices in it, and large ships and merchants. And so I think it must be the island of Cipango (Japan), of which they tell such wonders." The record, under date of Sunday, 28th of October, states: "Continued for the nearest land of Cuba, and entered a beautiful estuary, clear of rocks and other dangers. The mouth of the estuary had twelve fathoms depth, and it was wide enough for a ship to work into." Students have disagreed regarding the first Cuban port entered by Columbus. There is general acceptance of October 28 as the date of arrival. Some contend that on that day he entered Nipe Bay, while others, and apparently the greater number, locate the spot somewhat to the west of Nuevitas. Wherever he first landed on it, there is agreement that he called the island Juana, in honor of Prince Juan, taking possession "in the name of Christ, Our Lady, and the reigning Sovereigns of Spain."

His record of the landing place is obscure. It is known that he sailed some leagues beyond it, to the westward. While on board his caravel, on his homeward voyage, he wrote a letter to his friend, Don Rafael Sanchez, "Treasurer of their most Serene Highnesses," in which the experience is described. The original letter is lost, but it was translated into Latin and published in Barcelona in the following year, 1493. While the Latin form is variously translated into English, the general tenor of all is the same. He wrote: "When I arrived at Juana (Cuba), I sailed along the coast to the west, discovering so great an extent of land that I could not imagine it to be an island, but the continent of Cathay. I did not, however, discover upon the coast any large cities, all we saw being a few villages and farms, with the inhabitants of which we could not obtain any communication, they flying at our approach. I continued my course, still expecting to meet with some town or city, but after having gone a great distance and not meeting with any, and finding myself proceeding toward the north, which I was desirous, to avoid on account of the cold, and, moreover, meeting with a contrary wind, I determined to return to the south, and therefore put about and sailed back to a harbor which I had before observed." That the actual landing was at or near the present port of Nuevitas seems to be generally accepted.

Columbus appears to have been greatly impressed by the beauty of the island. In his *Life of Columbus*, Washington Irving says: "From his continual remarks on the beauty of scenery, and from his evident delight in rural sounds and objects, he appears to have been extremely open to those happy influences, exercised over some spirits, by the graces and wonders of nature. He gives utterance to these feelings with characteristic enthusiasm, and at the same time with the artlessness and simplicity of diction of a child. When speaking of some lovely scene among the groves, or along the flowery shores of these favored islands, he says, "One could live there forever." Cuba broke upon him like an elysium. "It is the most beautiful island," he says, "that ever eyes beheld, full of excellent ports and profound rivers." A little discount must be made on such a statement. Granting all that is to be said of Cuba's scenic charms, some allowance is to be made for two influences. One is Don Cristobal's exuberance, and the other is the fact that when one has been knocking about, as he had been, for nearly three months on the open sea and among low-lying and sandy islands and keys, any land, verdure clad and hilly, is a picture of Paradise. Many people need only two or three days at sea to reach a similar conclusion. In his letter to Luis de Santangel, Columbus says: "All these countries are of surpassing excellence, and in particular Juana (Cuba,), which contains abundance of fine harbors, excelling any in Christendom, as also many large and beautiful rivers. The land is high, and exhibits chains of tall mountains which seem to reach to the skies and surpass beyond comparison the isle of Cetrefrey (Sicily). These display themselves in all manner of beautiful shapes. They are accessible in every part, and covered with a vast variety of lofty trees which it appears to me never lose their foliage. Some were covered with blossoms, some with fruit, and others in different stages according to their nature. There are palm trees of six or eight sorts. Beautiful forests of pines are likewise found, and fields of vast extent. Here are also honey and fruits of thousand sorts, and birds of every variety."

Having landed at this indefinitely located point, Columbus, believing that he had reached the region he was seeking, despatched messengers to the interior to open communication with some high official of Cathay, in which country he supposed himself to be, the idea of Cipango apparently having been abandoned. "Many at the present day," says Washington Irving, "will smile at this embassy to a naked savage chieftain in the interior of Cuba, in mistake for an Asiatic monarch; but such was the singular nature of this voyage, a continual series of golden dreams, and all interpreted by the deluding volume of Marco Polo." But the messengers went on their journey, and proceeded inland some thirty or forty miles. There they came upon a village of about fifty huts and a population of about a thousand. They were able to communicate only by signs, and it is quite certain that the replies of the natives were as little understood by the messengers as the questions were by the natives. The messengers sought something about which the natives knew little or nothing. The communications were interpreted through the medium of imagination and desire. Nothing accomplished, the commission returned and made its disappointing report. Washington Irving thus describes the further proceedings: "The report of the envoys put an end to the many splendid fancies of Columbus, about the barbaric prince and his capital. He was cruising, however, in a region of enchantment, in which pleasing chimeras started up at every step, exercising by turns a power over his imagination. During the absence of the emissaries, the Indians had informed him, by signs, of a place to the eastward, where the people collected gold along the river banks by torchlight and afterward wrought it into bars with hammers. In speaking of this place they again used the words Babeque and Bohio, which he, as usual, supposed to be the proper names of islands or countries. His great object was to arrive at some opulent and civilized country of the East, with which he might establish commercial relations, and whence he might carry home a quantity of oriental merchandise as a rich trophy of his discovery. The season was advancing; the cool nights gave hints of approaching winter; he resolved, therefore, not to proceed farther to the north, nor to linger about uncivilized places which, at present, he had not the means of colonizing, but to return to the east-south-east, in quest of Babeque, which he trusted might prove some rich and civilized island on the coast of Asia." And so he sailed away for Hispaniola (Santo Domingo) which appears to have become, a little later, his favorite West Indian resort.

He began his eastward journey on November 12th. As he did not reach Cape Maisi, the eastern point of the island, until December 5th, he must have made frequent stops to examine the shore. Referring to one of the ports that he entered he wrote to the Spanish Sovereigns thus: "The amenity of this river, and the clearness of the water, through which the sand at the bottom may be seen; the multitude of palm trees of various forms, the highest and most beautiful that I have met with, and an infinity of other great and green trees; the birds in rich plumage and the verdure of the fields, render this country of such marvellous beauty that it surpasses all others in charms and graces, as the day doth the night in lustre. For which reason I often say to my people that, much as I endeavor to give a complete account of it to your majesties, my tongue cannot express the whole truth, nor my pen describe it; and I have been so overwhelmed at the sight of so much beauty that I have not known how to relate it."

Columbus made no settlement in Cuba; his part extends only to the discovery. On his second expedition, in the spring of 1494, he visited and explored the south coast as far west as the Isle of Pines, to which he gave the name *La Evangelista*. He touched the south coast again on his fourth voyage, in

1503. On his way eastward from his voyage of discovery on the coast of Central America, he missed his direct course to Hispaniola, and came upon the Cuban shore near Cape Cruz. He was detained there for some days by heavy weather and adverse winds, and sailed thence to his unhappy experience in Jamaica. The work of colonizing remained for others. Columbus died in the belief that he had discovered a part of the continent of Asia. That Cuba was only an island was determined by Sebastian de Ocampo who sailed around it in 1508. Baron Humboldt, who visited Cuba in 1801 and again in 1825, and wrote learnedly about it, states that "the first settlement of the whites occurred in 1511, when Velasquez, under orders from Don Diego Columbus, landed at Puerto de las Palmas, near Cape Maisi, and subjugated the Cacique Hatuey who had fled from Haiti to the eastern end of Cuba, where he became the chief of a confederation of several smaller native princes." This was, in fact, a military expedition composed of three hundred soldiers, with four vessels.

Hatuey deserves attention. His name is not infrequently seen in Cuba today, but it is probable that few visitors know whether it refers to a man, a bird, or a vegetable. He was the first Cuban hero of whom we have record, although the entire reliability of the record is somewhat doubtful. The notable historian of this period is Bartolome Las Casas, Bishop of Chiapa. He appears to have been a man of great worth, a very tender heart, and an imagination fully as vivid as that of Columbus. His sympathies were aroused by the tales of the exceeding brutality of many of the early Spanish voyagers in their relations with the natives. He went out to see for himself, and wrote voluminously of his experiences. He also wrote with exceeding frankness, and often with great indignation. He writes about Hatuey. The inference is that this Cacique, or chieftain, fled from Haiti to escape Spanish brutality, and even in fear of his life. There are other translations of Las Casas, but for this purpose choice has been made of one published in London about the year 1699. It is given thus:

"There happened divers things in this island (Cuba) that deserve to be remarked. A rich and potent Cacique named Hatuey was retired into the Isle of Cuba to avoid that Slavery and Death with which the Spaniards menaced him; and being informed that his persecutors were upon the point of landing in this Island, he assembled all his Subjects and Domestics together, and made a Speech unto them after this manner. "You know, (said he) the Report is spread abroad that the Spaniards are ready to invade this Island, and you are not ignorant of the ill usage our Friends and Countrymen have met with at their hands, and the cruelties they have committed at Haiti (so Hispaniola is called in their Language). They are now coming hither with a design to exercise the same Outrages and Persecutions upon us. Are you ignorant (says he) of the ill Intentions of the People of whom I am speaking? We know not (say they all with one voice) upon what account they come hither, but we know they are a very wicked and cruel People. I'll tell you then (replied the Cacique) that these Europeans worship a very covetous sort of God, so that it is difficult to satisfy him; to perform the Worship they render to this Idol, they will exact immense Treasures of us, and will use their utmost endeavors to reduce us to a miserable state of Slavery, or else put us to death." The historian leaves to the imagination and credulity of his readers the task of determining just where and how he got the full details of this speech and of the subsequent proceedings. The report of the latter may well be generally correct inasmuch as there were Spanish witnesses present, but the account of this oration, delivered prior to the arrival of the Spanish invaders, is clearly open to a suspicion that it may be more or less imaginary. But the historian continues: "Upon this he took a Box full of Gold and valuable Jewels which he had with him, and exposing it to their view: Here is (said he) the God of the Spaniards, whom we must honor with our Sports and Dances, to see if we can appease him and render him propitious to us; that so he may command the Spaniards not to offer us any injury. They all applauded this Speech, and fell a leaping and dancing around the Box, till they had quite tired and spent themselves. After which the Cacique Hatuey resuming his Discourse, continued to speak to them in these terms: If we keep this God (says he) till he's taken away from us, he'll certainly cause our lives to be taken away from us; and therefore I am of opinion it will be the best way to cast him into the river. They all approved of this Advice, and went all together with one accord to throw this pretended God into the River."

But the Spaniards came and encountered the resistance of Hatuey and his followers. The invaders were victorious, and Hatuey was captured and burned alive. Las Casas relates that while the poor wretch was in the midst of the flames, tied to a stake, "a certain Franciscan Friar of great Piety and Virtue, took upon him to speak to him of God and our Religion, and to explain to him some Articles of Catholic Faith, of which he had never heard a word before, promising him Eternal Life if he would believe and threatening him with Eternal Torment if he continued obstinate in his Infidelity. Hatuey reflecting on the matter, as much as the Place and Condition in which he was would permit, asked the Friar that instructed him, whether the Gate of Heaven was open to Spaniards; and being answered that such of them as were good men might hope for entrance there: the Cacique, without any farther deliberation, told him that he had no mind to go to heaven for fear of meeting with such cruel and wicked Company as they were; but he would much rather choose to go to Hell where he might be delivered from the troublesome sight of such kind of People." And so died the Cacique Hatuey. Four hundred years later, the Cuban Government named a gunboat *Hatuey*, in his honor.

The Velasquez expedition, in the following year, founded Baracoa, now a small city on the northern coast near the eastern extremity of the island. It is a spot of exceeding scenic charm. It was established as the capital city, but it held that honor for a few years only. In 1514 and 1515, settlements were established at what is now Santiago, at Sancti Spiritus, Trinidad, and Batabano. The latter was originally called San Cristobal de la Habana, the name being transferred to the present city, on the north coast, in 1519. It displaced the name Puerto de Carenas given to the present Havana by Ocampo, who careened his vessels there in 1508. Baracoa was made the seat of a bishopric, and a cathedral was begun, in 1518. In 1522, both the capital and the bishopric were transferred to

Santiago, a location more readily accessible from the new settlements on the south coast, and also from Jamaica which was then included in the diocese. Cuba, at about this period, was the point of departure for an important expedition. In 1517, de Cordoba, with three vessels and 110 soldiers, was sent on an expedition to the west for further and more northerly exploration of the land discovered by Columbus in 1503. The coast from Panama to Honduras had been occupied. The object of this expedition was to learn what lay to the northward. The result was the discovery of Yucatan. Cordoba returned to die of wounds received in a battle. A second and stronger expedition was immediately despatched. This rounded the peninsula and followed the coast as far as the present city of Vera Cruz. In 1518, Hernan Cortez was *alcalde*, or mayor, of Santiago de Cuba. On November 18, of that year, he sailed from that port in command of an expedition for the conquest of Mexico, finally effected in 1521, after one of the most romantic campaigns in the history of warfare. All that, however, is a story in which Cuba has no place except that of the starting point and base of the expedition. There is another story of the same kind, a few years later. The first discovery of Florida is somewhat uncertain. It appears on an old Spanish map dated 1502. Following the expedition of Ponce de Leon, in 1513, and of Murielo, in 1516, Narvaez headed an expedition from Cuba in 1528 with some three hundred freebooters. They landed in Florida, where almost the entire band was, very properly, destroyed by the Indians. In 1539, de Soto sailed from Havana, with five hundred and seventy men and two hundred and twenty-three horses, for an extended exploration. They wandered for three years throughout what is now the southern part of the United States from Georgia and South Carolina westward to Arkansas and Missouri. After a series of almost incredible experiences, de Soto died in 1542, on the banks of the Mississippi River at a point probably not far from the Red River. These and other expeditions, from Cuba and from Mexico, to what is now territory of the United States, produced no permanent results. No gold was found.

Of the inhabitants of Cuba, as found by the Spaniards, comparatively little is recorded. They seem to have been a somewhat negative people, generally described as docile, gentle, generous, and indolent. Their garments were quite limited, and their customs altogether primitive. They disappear from Cuba's story in its earliest chapters. Very little is known of their numbers. Some historians state that, in the days of Columbus, the island had a million inhabitants, but this is obviously little if anything more than a rough guess. Humboldt makes the following comment: "No means now exist to arrive at a knowledge of the population of Cuba in the time of Columbus; but how can we admit what some otherwise judicious historians state, that when the island of Cuba was conquered in 1511, it contained a million inhabitants of whom only 14,000 remained in 1517. The statistical information which we find in the writings of Las Casas is filled with contradictions." Forty years or so later the Dominican friar, Luis Bertram, on his return to Spain, predicted that "the 200,000 Indians now in the island of Cuba, will perish, victims to the cruelty of the Europeans." Yet Gomara stated that there was not an Indian in Cuba after

1553. Whatever the exact truth regarding numbers, it is evident that they disappeared rapidly, worked to death by severe task-masters. The institution of African slavery, to take the place of the inefficient and fast disappearing native labor, had its beginning in 1521. Baron Humboldt states that from that time until 1790, the total number of African negroes imported as slaves was 90,875. In the next thirty years, the business increased rapidly, and Humboldt estimates the total arrivals, openly entered and smuggled in, from 1521 to 1820, as 372,449. Mr. J.S. Thrasher, in a translation of Humboldt's work, issued in 1856, added a footnote showing the arrivals up to 1854 as 644,000. A British official authority, at the same period, gives the total as a little less than 500,000. The exact number is not important. The institution on a large scale, in its relation to the total number of whites, was a fact.

It is, of course, quite impossible even today to argue the question of slavery. To many, the offence lies in the mere fact; to others, it lies in the operation of the system. At all events, the institution is no longer tolerated in any civilized country. While some to whom the system itself was a bitter offence have found much to criticize in its operation in Cuba, the general opinion of observers appears to be that it was there notably free from the brutality usually supposed to attend it. The Census Report of 1899, prepared under the auspices of the American authorities, states that "while it was fraught with all the horrors of this nefarious business elsewhere, the laws for the protection of slaves were unusually humane. Almost from the beginning, slaves had a right to purchase their freedom or change their masters, and long before slavery was abolished they could own property and contract marriage. As a result, the proportion of free colored to slaves has always been large." Humboldt, who studied the institution while it was most extensive, states that "the position of the free negroes in Cuba is much better than it is elsewhere, even among those nations which have for ages flattered themselves as being most advanced in civilization." The movement for the abolition of slavery had its beginning in 1815, with the treaty of Vienna, to which Spain was a party. Various acts in the same direction appear in the next fifty years. The Moret law, enacted in 1870 by the Spanish Cortes, provided for gradual abolition in Spain's dominions, and a law of 1880, one of the results of the Ten Years' War, definitely abolished the system. Traces of it remained, however, until about 1887, when it may be regarded as having become extinct forever in Cuba.

For the first two hundred and fifty years of Cuba's history, the city of Havana appears as the special centre of interest. There was growth in other sections, but it was slow, for reasons that will be explained elsewhere. In 1538, Havana was attacked and totally destroyed by a French privateer. Hernando de Soto, then Governor of the island, at once began the construction of defences that are now one of the special points of interest in the city. The first was the Castillo de la Fuerza. In 1552, Havana became the capital city. In 1555, it was again attacked, and practically destroyed, including the new fortress, by French buccaneers. Restoration was effected as rapidly as possible. In 1589, La Fuerza was enlarged, and the construction of the Morro and of La Punta, the fortress at the foot of the Prado, was begun. The old city wall, of which portions still remain, was of a later period. Despite these precautions, the city was repeatedly attacked by pirates and privateers. Some reference to these experiences will be made in a special chapter on the city. The slow progress of the island is shown by the fact that an accepted official report gives the total population in 1775 as 171,620, of whom less than 100,000 were white. The absence of precious metals is doubtless the main reason for the lack of Spanish interest in the development of the country. For a long time after the occupation, the principal industry was cattle raising. Agriculture, the production of sugar, tobacco, coffee, and other crops, on anything properly to be regarded as a commercial scale, was an experience of later years. The reason for this will be found in the mistaken colonial policy of Spain, a policy the application of which, in a far milder manner, cost England its richest colony in the Western Hemisphere, and which, in the first quarter of the 19th Century, cost Spain all of its possessions in this half of the world, with the exception of Cuba and Porto Rico.

II

NEW CUBA

While there is no point in Cuba's history that may be said to mark a definite division between the Old Cuba and the New Cuba, the beginning of the 19th Century may be taken for that purpose. Cuba's development dragged for two hundred and fifty years. The population increased slowly and industry lagged. For this, Spain's colonial policy was responsible. But it was the policy of the time, carried out more or less effectively by all nations having colonies. England wrote it particularly into her Navigation Acts of 1651, 1660, and 1663, and supported it by later Acts. While not rigorously enforced, and frequently evaded by the American colonists, the system at last proved so offensive that the colonists revolted in 1775. Most of Spain's colonies in the Western Hemisphere, for the same reason, declared and maintained their independence in the first quarter of the 19th Century. At the bottom of Cuba's several little uprisings, and at the bottom of its final revolt in 1895, lay the same cause of offence. In those earlier years, it was held that colonies existed solely for the benefit of the mother-country. In 1497, almost at the very beginning of Spain's colonial enterprises in the New World, a royal decree was issued under which the exclusive privilege to carry on trade with the colonies was granted to the port of Seville. This monopoly was transferred to the port of Cadiz in 1717, but it continued, in somewhat modified form in later years, until Spain had no colonies left.

While Santiago was the capital of the island, from 1522 to 1552, trade between Spain and the island could be carried on only through that port. When Havana became the capital, in 1552, the exclusive privilege of trade was transferred to that city. With the exception of the years 1762 and 1763, when the British occupied Havana and declared it open to all trade, the commerce of the island could only be done through Havana with Seville, until 1717, and afterward with Cadiz. Baracoa, or Santiago, or Trinidad, or any other Cuban city, could not send goods to Santander, or Malaga, or Barcelona, or any other Spanish market, or receive goods directly from them. The law prohibited trade between Cuba and all other countries, and limited all trade between the island and the mother-country to the port of Havana, at one end, and to Seville or Cadiz, according to the time of the control of those ports, at the other end. Even intercolonial commerce was prohibited. At times, and for brief periods, the system was modified to the extent of special trade licences, and, occasionally, by international treaties. But the general system of trade restriction was maintained throughout all of Spain's colonial experience. Between 1778 and 1803, most of Cuba's ports were opened to trade with Spain. The European wars of the early years of the 19th Century led to modification of the trade laws, but in 1809 foreign commerce with Spanish American ports was again prohibited. A few years later, Spain had lost nearly all its American colonies. A new plan was adopted in 1818. Under that, Spain sought to hold the trade of Cuba and Porto

Rico by tariffs so highly favorable to merchandise from the mother-country as to be effectively prohibitive with regard to many products from other countries. This, in general outline, is the cause of Cuba's slow progress until the 19th Century, and the explanation of its failure to make more rapid progress during that century.

Naturally, under such conditions, bribery of officials and smuggling became active and lucrative enterprises. It may be said, in strict confidence between writer and reader, that Americans were frequently the parties of the other part in these transactions. In search through a considerable number of American histories, I have been unable to find definite references to trade with Cuba, yet there seems to be abundant reason for belief that such trade was carried on. There are many references to trade with the West Indies as far back as 1640 and even a year or two earlier, but allusions to trade with Cuba do not appear, doubtless for the reason that it was contraband, a violation of both Spanish and British laws. There was evidently some relaxation toward the close of the 18th Century. There are no records of the commerce of the American colonies, and only fragmentary records between 1776 and 1789. The more elaborate records of 1789 and following years show shipments of fish, whale oil, spermaceti candles, lumber, staves and heading, and other articles to the "Spanish West Indies," in which group Cuba was presumably included. The records of the time are somewhat unreliable. It was a custom for the small vessels engaged in that trade to take out clearance papers for the West Indies. The cargo might be distributed in a number of ports, and the return cargo might be similarly collected. For the year 1795, the records of the United States show total imports from the Spanish West Indies as valued at $1,740,000, and exports to that area as valued at $1,390,000. In 1800, the imports were $10,588,000, and the exports $8,270,000. Just how much of this was trade with Cuba, does not appear. Because of the trade increase at that time, and because of other events that, soon afterward, brought Cuba into more prominent notice, this period has been chosen as the line of division between the Old and the New Cuba.

Compared with the wonderful fertility of Cuba, New England is a sterile area. Yet in 1790, a hundred and seventy years after its settlement, the latter had a population a little exceeding a million, while the former, in 1792, or two hundred and eighty years after its occupation, is officially credited with a population of 272,300. Of these, 153,559 were white and 118,741 were colored. Several forces came into operation at this time, and population increased rapidly, to 572,363 in 1817, and to 704,465 in 1827. In 1841, it was a little more than a million. But the increase in colored population, by the importation of African slaves, outstripped the increase by the whites. In 1841, the population was divided into 418,291 whites and 589,333 colored. The importation of slaves having declined, the year 1861 shows a white preponderance, since continued and substantially increased. Among the forces contributing to Cuba's rapid growth during this period were a somewhat greater freedom of trade; the revolution in the neighboring island of Haiti and Santo Domingo, that had its beginning in 1791 and culminated, some ten years later, in the rule of Toussaint

L'Ouverture; and an increased demand for sugar. One result of the Haitian disorder was the arrival, in eastern Cuba, of a large number of exiles and emigrants who established extensive coffee plantations. During the first hundred and fifty years of Cuba's history, the principal industry of the island was cattle raising, aside from the domestic industry of food supply. The proprietors lived, usually, in the cities and maintained their vast estates in the neighborhood. To this, later on, were added the production of honey and wax and the cultivation of tobacco. With the period now under consideration, there came the expansion of the coffee and sugar industries. The older activities do not appear to have been appreciably lessened; the others were added on.

Europe and the Western Hemisphere were at that time in a state of general upheaval and rearrangement. Following the American Revolution, there came the French Revolution; the Napoleonic Wars; the war of 1812 between the United States and England; and the general revolt of the Spanish colonies. The world was learning new lessons, adopting new policies, in which the Spanish colonial system was a blunder the folly of which Spain did not even then fully realize. Yet from it all, by one means and another, Cuba benefited. Spain was fortunate in its selection of Governors-General sent out at this time. Luis de Las Casas, who arrived in 1790, is credited with much useful work. He improved roads and built bridges; established schools and the *Casa de Beneficencia*, still among the leading institutions in Havana; paved the streets of Havana; improved as far as he could the commercial conditions; and established the *Sociedad Patriotica*, sometimes called the *Sociedad Economica*, an organization that has since contributed immeasurably to Cuba's welfare and progress. He was followed by others whose rule was creditable. But the principal evils, restricted commerce and burdensome taxation, were not removed, although world conditions practically compelled some modification of the commercial regulations. In 1801 the ports of the island were thrown open to the trade of friendly and neutral nations. Eight years later, foreign commerce was again prohibited. In 1818, a new system was established, that of a tariff so highly favorable to merchandise from Spain that it was by no means unusual for goods to be shipped to that country, even from the United States, and from there reshipped to Cuba. Changes in the rates were made from time to time, but the system of heavy discrimination in favor of Spanish goods in Spanish ships continued until the equalization of conditions under the order of the Government of Intervention, in 1899.

In his book published in 1840, Mr. Turnbull states that "the mercantile interests of the island have been greatly promoted by the relaxation of those restrictive regulations which under the old peninsular system bound down all foreign commerce with the colonies of Spain, and laid it prostrate at the feet of the mother-country. It cannot be said that the sound principles of free trade, in any large or extended sense of the term, have been recognized or acted upon even at the single port of Havana. The discriminating duties imposed by the supreme government of Madrid on the natural productions, manufactures, and shipping of foreign countries, in contradistinction to those of Spain, are so stringent and so onerous as altogether to exclude the idea of anything approaching to commercial freedom. There is no longer, it is true, any absolute prohibition, but in many cases the distinguishing duties are so heavy as to defeat their own object, and, in place of promoting the interests of the mother-country, have had little other effect than the establishment of an extensive and ruinous contraband." Under such conditions as those existing in Cuba, from its beginning practically until the establishment of its political independence, industrial development and commercial expansion are more than difficult.

One of the natural results of such a system appeared in the activities of smugglers. The extent to which that industry was carried on cannot, of course, be even guessed. Some have estimated that the merchandise imported in violation of the laws equalled in value the merchandise entered at the custom houses. An official publication (American) states that "from smuggling on a large scale and privateering to buccaneering and piracy is not a long step, and under the name of privateers French, Dutch, English, and American smugglers and buccaneers swarmed the Caribbean Sea and the Gulf of Mexico for more than two centuries, plundering Spanish *flotas* and attacking colonial settlements. Among the latter, Cuba was the chief sufferer." Had Cuba's coasts been made to order for the purpose, they could hardly have been better adapted to the uses of smugglers. Off shore, for more than half its coast line, both north and south, are small islands and keys with narrow and shallow passages between them, thus making an excellent dodging area for small boats if pursued by revenue vessels. Thoroughly familiar with these entrances and hiding places, smugglers could land their goods almost at will with little danger of detection or capture.

Another heavy handicap on the economic progress of the island appears in the system of taxation. Regarding this system, the Census of 1899 reports as follows:

"Apart from imports and exports, taxes were levied on real and personal property and on industries and commerce of all kinds. Every profession, art, or manual occupation contributed its quota, while, as far back as 1638, seal and stamp taxes were established on all judicial business and on all kinds of petitions and claims made to official corporations, and subsequently on all bills and accounts. These taxes were in the form of stamps on official paper and at the date of American occupation the paper cost from 35 cents to $3 a sheet. On deeds, wills, and other similar documents the paper cost from 35 cents to $37.50 per sheet, according to the value of the property concerned. Failure to use even the lowest-priced paper involved a fine of $50.

"There was also a municipal tax on the slaughter of cattle for the market. This privilege was sold by the municipal council to the highest bidder, with the result that taxes were assessed on all animals slaughtered, whether for the market or for private consumption, with a corresponding increase in the price of meat.

"Another tax established in 1528, called the *derecho de avería*, required the payment of 20 ducats ($16) by every person, bond or free, arriving in the island. In 1665 this tax was increased to $22, and continued in force to 1765, thus retarding immigration, and, to that extent, the increase of population, especially of the laboring class.

"An examination of these taxes will show their excessive, arbitrary, and unscientific character, and how they operated to discourage Cubans from owning property or engaging in many industrial pursuits tending to benefit them and to promote the material improvement of the island.

"Taxes on real estate were estimated by the tax inspector on the basis of its rental or productive capacity, and varied from 4 to 12 per cent. Similarly, a nominal municipal tax of 25 per cent was levied on the estimated profits of all industries and commerce, and on the income derived from all professions, manual occupations, or agencies, the collector receiving 6 per cent of all taxes assessed. Much unjust discrimination was made against Cubans in determining assessable values and in collecting the taxes, and it is said that bribery in some form was the only effective defense against the most flagrant impositions."

Some of the experiences of this period will be considered in special chapters on Cuba's alleged revolutions and on the relations of the United States to Cuba and its affairs. One point may be noted here. The wave of republicanism that swept over a considerable part of Europe and over the Western Hemisphere, from 1775 to 1825 had its direct influence in Spain, and an influence only less direct in Cuba. In 1812, Spain became a constitutional monarchy. It is true that the institution had only a brief life, but the sentiment that lay beneath it persisted and had been repeatedly a cause of disturbance on the Peninsula. Something of the same sentiment pervaded Cuba and excited ambitions, not for national independence, but for some participation in government. A royal decree, in 1810, gave Cuba representation in the Cortes, and two deputies from the island took part in framing the Constitution of 1812. This recognition of Cuba lasted for only two years, the Constitution being abrogated in 1814, but it was restored in 1820, only to cease again three years later. Representatives were again admitted to the Cortes in 1834, and again excluded in 1837. The effect of all this was, perhaps, psychological rather than practical, but it gave rise to a new mental attitude and to some change in conduct. The effect appears in the numerous recurrences of open protest and passive resistance in the place of the earlier submission. Writing in 1855, Mr. J.S. Thrasher stated that "the essential political elements of the island are antagonistic to those of the mother-country. While the Cortes and the crown have frequently declared that Cuba does not form an integral part of the Spanish monarchy, but must be governed by special laws not applicable to Spain, and persist in ruling her under the erroneous and unjust European colonial system, the growing wealth and increasing intelligence of the Cubans lead them to aspire to some share in the elimination of the political principles under which their own affairs shall be administered. A like antagonism exists in the economic relations of the two countries. While the people of Cuba are not averse to the raising of such revenue as may be required for the proper wants of the State, in the administration of which they may participate, they complain, with a feeling of national pride, that fiscal burdens of the most onerous kind are laid upon them for the expressed purpose of advancing interests which are in every sense opposed to their own. Thus, Spain imposes taxes to support a large army and navy, the principal object of which is to prevent any expression of the public will on the part of the people of Cuba. Another class of impositions have for their object the diversion of the trade of Cuba to channels which shall increase the profits of the agriculturists and mariners of Spain without regard to the interests of the people of the island."

Yet in spite of these severe restrictions and heavy burdens, Cuba shows a considerable progress during the first half of the century. It is far from easy to reach fair conclusions from contemporaneous writings. Naturally, Spanish officials and Spanish writers strove to make the best possible case for Spain, its policies and its conduct. The press of the island was either under official control or stood in fear of official reprisals. The Cuban side, naturally partisan, appears to have been presented chiefly by fugitive pamphlets, more or less surreptitiously printed and distributed, usually the product of political extremists. Among these was a man of marked ability and of rare skill in the use of language. He was Don Antonio Saco, known in Cuba as the "Immortal Saco." In a letter written to a friend, in 1846, he says, "The tyranny of our mother-country, today most acute, will have this result—that within a period of time not very remote the Cubans will be compelled to take up arms to banish her." That British observers and most American observers should take the side of the Cubans is altogether natural. Writing in 1854, Mr. M.M. Ballou, in his *History of Cuba*, says: "The Cubans owe all the blessings they enjoy to Providence alone (so to speak), while the evils which they suffer are directly referable to the oppression of the home government. Nothing short of a military despotism could maintain the connection of such an island with a mother-country more than three thousand miles distant; and accordingly we find the captain-general of Cuba invested with unlimited power. He is, in fact, a viceroy appointed by the crown of Spain, and accountable only to the reigning sovereign for his administration of the colony. His rule is absolute; he has the power of life and death and liberty in his hands. He can, by his arbitrary will, send into exile any person whatever, be his name or rank what it may, whose residence in the island he considers prejudicial to the royal interest, even if he has committed no overt act. He can suspend the operation of the laws and ordinances, if he sees fit to do so; can destroy or confiscate property; and, in short, the island may be said to be perpetually in a state of siege."

The student or the reader may take his choice. On one side are Spanish statements, official and semi-official, and on the other side, Cuban statements no less partisan. The facts appear to support the Cuban argument. In spite of the severe restrictions and the heavy burdens, Cuba shows a notable progress during the 19th Century. Governors came and went, some very good and others very bad. There were a hundred of them from 1512 to 1866, and thirty-six more from 1866 to 1899, the average term of service for the entire number being a little less than three years. On the whole, the most notable of the group of 19th Century incumbents was Don Miguel Tacon, who ruled from June 1, 1834, until April 16, 1838. His record would seem to place him quite decidedly in the "reactionary" class, but he was a man of action who left behind him monuments that remain to his credit even now. One historian, Mr. Kimball, who wrote in 1850, describes him as one in whom short-sightedness, narrow views, and jealous and weak mind, were joined to an uncommon stubbornness of character. Another, Mr. M.M. Ballou, says that "probably of all the governors-general that have filled the post in Cuba none is better known abroad, or has left more monuments to his enterprise, than Tacon. His reputation at Havana (this was written 1854) is of a somewhat doubtful character; for, though he followed out with energy various improvements, yet his modes of procedure were so violent that he was an object of terror to the people generally, rather than of gratitude. He vastly improved the appearance of the capital and its vicinity, built the new prison, rebuilt the governor's palace, constructed a military road to the neighboring forts, erected a spacious theatre and market house, arranged a new public walk, and opened a vast parade ground without the city walls, thus laying the foundation of the new city which has now sprung up in this formerly desolate suburb. He suppressed the gaming houses and rendered the streets, formerly infested with robbers, as secure as those of Boston or New York." Another writer, Mr. Samuel Hazard, in 1870, says: "Of all the governors who have been in command of the island Governor Tacon seems to have been the best, doing the most to improve the island, and particularly Havana; making laws, punishing offences, and establishing some degree of safety for its inhabitants. It is reported of him that he is said, like the great King Alfred, to have promised the Cubans that they should be able to leave their purses of money on the public highway without fear of having them stolen. At all events, his name is cherished by every Cuban for the good he has done, and *paseos*, theatres, and monuments bear his great name in Havana." The Tacon theatre is now the Nacional, and the Paseo Tacon is now Carlos III. The "new prison" is the *Carcel*, or jail, at the northern end of the Prado, near the fortress of La Punta. Don Miguel may have been disliked for his methods and his manners, but he certainly did much to make his rule memorable.

There is no reliable information that shows the progress of the island during the 19th Century. Even the census figures are questioned. A reported 432,000 total population in 1804 is evidently no more than an estimate, yet it is very likely not far from the actual. Concerning their distribution throughout the island, and the number engaged in different occupations, there are no records. There are no acceptable figures regarding the respective numbers of whites and blacks. Nor is there any record of the population in 1895, the year of the war for independence. From the definite tabulation, under American auspices, in 1899, showing 1,576,797, it has been estimated that the number in 1895, was a little less than 1,800,000, the difference being represented by the disasters of the war, by the result of reconcentration, and by departures during the disturbance. The general result seems to be that the population was practically quadrupled. A somewhat rough approximation would show the blacks as multiplied by three, to an 1899 total of 505,000, with the whites multiplied by four, to a total of 1,067,000. Nor are there figures of trade that afford any proper clue to the growth of industry and commerce. There are records of imports and exports from about 1850 onward, but before that time the matter of contraband trade introduces an element of uncertainty. An American official pamphlet on Cuban trade carries the statement, "the ascertainment of full and exact details of the commerce of Cuba prior to the close of Spanish dominion in the island is an impossibility. The Spanish authorities, as a rule, published no complete returns of Cuban trade, either foreign or domestic. Except with regard to Spain and the United States, most of the existing commercial statistics of Cuba, prior to 1899, are fragmentary and merely approximative. Spain and the United States have always kept a separate and distinct trade account with Cuba; but the United Kingdom, France, Germany, and other European countries excepting Spain, formerly merged their statistics of trade with Cuba in one general item embracing Cuba and Porto Rico, under the heading of "Spanish West Indies." Since 1899, however, all the Powers have kept separate accounts with Cuba, and the statistics of the Cuban Republic have been reasonably full and accurate."

Cuba's recorded imports in 1894 show a total value of $90,800,000, and exports show a value of $102,000,000. Writing about the year 1825, Humboldt says: "It is more than probable that the imports of the whole island, licit and contraband, estimated at the actual value of the goods and the slaves, amount, at the present time, to fifteen or sixteen millions of dollars, of which barely three or four millions are re-exported." The same authority gives the probable exports of that time as about $12,500,000. The trade at the beginning of the century must have been far below this. The official figures for 1851 show total imports amounting to $34,000,000, and exports to $33,000,000, but the accuracy of the figures is open to question. The more important fact is that of a very large gain in population and in production. The coffee industry, that assumed important proportions during a part of the first half of the century, gradually declined for the reason that sugar became a much more profitable crop. Now, Cuba imports most of its coffee from Porto Rico. Because of its convenience as a contraband article, there are no reliable figures of the tobacco output. Prior to 1817, the commodity was, for much of the time, a crown monopoly and, for the remainder of the time, a monopoly concession to private companies. In that year, cultivation and trade became free, subject to a tax on each planter of one-twentieth of his production.

As we shall see, in another chapter, Cuba at last wearied of Spanish exactions and revolted as did the United States, weary of British rule and British exactions and restrictions, more than a hundred years earlier.

III

THE COUNTRY

Description of the physical features of a country seldom makes highly entertaining reading, but it seems a necessary part of a book of this kind. Some readers may find interest if not entertainment in such a review. The total area of the island, including a thousand or more adjacent islands, islets, and keys, is given as 44,164 square miles, a little less than the area of Pennsylvania and a little more than that of Ohio or Tennessee. Illustration of its shape by some familiar object is difficult, although various comparisons have been attempted. Some old Spanish geographers gave the island the name of *La Lengua de Pajaro*, "the bird's tongue." Mr. M.M. Ballou likened it to "the blade of a Turkish scimitar slightly curved back, or approaching the form of a long, narrow, crescent." Mr. Robert T. Hill holds that it "resembles a great hammer-headed shark, the head of which forms the straight, south coast of the east end of the island, from which the sinuous body extends westward. This analogy is made still more striking by two long, finlike strings of keys, or islets, which extend backward along the opposite coasts, parallel to the main body of the island." But all such comparisons call for a lively imagination. It might be likened to the curving handles of a plow attached to a share, or to any one of a dozen things that it does not at all clearly resemble. Regarding the Oriente coast, from Cape Cruz to Cape Maisi, as a base, from that springs a long and comparatively slender arm that runs northwesterly for five hundred miles to the vicinity of Havana. There, the arm, somewhat narrowed, turns downward in a generally southwestern direction for about two hundred miles. The total length of the island, from Cape Maisi on the east to Cape San Antonio on the west, is about seven hundred and thirty miles. Its width varies from a maximum, in Oriente Province, of about one hundred and sixty miles, to a minimum, in Havana Province, of about twenty-two miles. It has a general coast line of about twenty-two hundred miles, or, following all its sinuosities, of about seven thousand miles. Its north coast is, for much of its length, steep and rocky. Throughout the greater part of the middle provinces, there is a border of coral reefs and small islands. At the western end, the north coast is low, rising gradually to the eastward. At the eastern end, the northern coast is abrupt and rugged, rising in a series of hills to the elevations in the interior. Westward from Cape Maisi to Cape Cruz, on the south coast, and immediately along the shore line, runs a mountain range. From here westward, broken by an occasional hill or bluff, the coast is low and marshy.

Probably the best description of the topography and the orography of the island yet presented is that given by Mr. Robert T. Hill, of the United States Geological Survey. In his book on Cuba and other islands of the West Indies, Mr. Hill says:

"As regards diversity of relief, Cuba's eastern end is mountainous, with summits standing high above the adjacent sea; its middle portion is wide, consisting of gently sloping plains, well-drained, high above the sea, and broken here and there by low, forest-clad hills; and its western third is a picturesque region of mountains, with fertile slopes and valleys, of different structure and less altitude than those of the east. Over the whole is a mantle of tender vegetation, rich in every hue that a flora of more than three thousand species can give, and kept green by mists and gentle rains. Indenting the rock-bound coasts are a hundred pouch-shaped harbors such as are but rarely found in the other islands and shores of the American Mediterranean.

"But, at the outset the reader should dispossess his mind of any preconceived idea that the island of Cuba is in any sense a physical unit. On the contrary, it presents a diversity of topographic, climatic, and cultural features, which, as distributed, divide the island into at least three distinct natural provinces, for convenience termed the eastern, central, and western regions. The distinct types of relief include regions of high mountains, low hills, dissected plateaus, intermontane valleys, and coastal swamps. With the exception of a strip of the south-central coast, the island, as a whole, stands well above the sea, is thoroughly drained, and presents a rugged aspect when viewed from the sea. About one-fourth of the total area is mountainous, three-fifths are rolling plain, valleys, and gentle arable slopes, and the remainder is swampy.

"The island border on the north presents a low cliff topography, with a horizontal sky-line from Matanzas westward, gradually decreasing from five hundred feet at Matanzas to one hundred feet on the west. The coast of the east end is abrupt and rugged, presenting on both the north and south sides a series of remarkable terraces, rising in stair-like arrangement to six hundred feet or more, representing successive pauses or stages in the elevation of the island above the sea, and constituting most striking scenic features. About one-half the Cuban coast is bordered by keys, which are largely old reef rock, the creations of the same coral-builders that may now be seen through the transparent waters still at work on the modern shallows, decking the rocks and sands with their graceful and many colored tufts of animal foliage."

Mr. Hill summarizes the general appearance of the island, thus: "Santiago de Cuba (now called Oriente) is predominantly a mountainous region of high relief, especially along the coasts, with many interior valleys. Puerto Principe (now Camaguey) and Santa Clara are broken regions of low mountain relief, diversified by extensive valleys. Matanzas and Havana are vast stretches of level cultivated plain, with only a few hills of relief. Pinar del Rio is centrally mountainous, with fertile coastward slopes." The notable elevations of the island are the Cordilleras de los Organos, or Organ Mountains, in Pinar del Rio, of which an eastward extension appears in the Tetas de Managua, the Arcas de Canasi, the Escalera de Jaruco, the Pan de Matanzas, and other minor elevations in Havana and Matanzas Provinces. In Santa Clara and Camaguey, the range is represented by crest lines and plateaus along the north shore, and finally runs into the hill and mountain maze of Oriente. In the south-central section of the island, a somewhat isolated group of elevations appears, culminating in El Potrerillo at a height of nearly 3,000 feet. In Oriente, immediately along the south coast line, is the precipitous Sierra Maestra, reaching its greatest altitude in the Pico del Turquino, with an elevation of approximately 8,500 feet. Another elevation, near Santiago, known as La Gran Piedra, is estimated at 5,200 feet. All these heights are densely wooded. From the tops of some of them, east, west, and central, the views are marvellously beautiful, but the summits of most are reached only with considerable difficulty. One of the most notable of these view points, and one of the most easily reached, is the height immediately behind the city of Matanzas, overlooking the famous Yumuri valley. The valley is a broad, shallow bowl, some five or six miles in diameter, enclosed by steeply sloping walls of five to six hundred feet in height. Through it winds the Yumuri River. It is best seen in the early forenoon, or the late afternoon, when there come the shadows and the lights that are largely killed by the more vertical rays of a midday sun. At those hours, it is a scene of entrancing loveliness. There are views, elsewhere, covering wider expanses, but none, I think, of equal beauty.

The vicinity of Matanzas affords a spectacle of almost enchantment for the sight-seer, and of deep interest for the geologist. Somewhat more than fifty years ago, an accident revealed the beautiful caves of Bellamar, two or three miles from the city, and easily reached by carriage. Caves ought to be cool. These are not, but they are well worth all the perspiration it costs to see them. They are a show place, and guides are always available. In size, the caverns are not comparable with the caves of Kentucky and Virginia, but they far excel in beauty. They are about three miles in extent, and their lower levels are said to be about five hundred feet from the surface. The rock is white limestone, in which are chambers and passage-ways, stalactites and stalagmites innumerable. These have their somewhat fantastic but not unfitting names, such as the Gothic Temple, the Altar, the Guardian Spirit, the Fountain of Snow, and Columbus' Mantle. The place has been called "a dream of fairyland," a fairly appropriate description. The colors are snow-white, pink, and shades of yellow, and many of the forms are wonderfully beautiful. There are many other caves in the island, like Cotilla, in the Guines region not far from Havana, others in the Cubitas Mountains in Camaguey Province, and still others in Oriente, but in comparison with Bellamar they are little else than holes in the ground. The trip through these remarkable aisles and chambers occupies some three or four hours.

Cuba is not big enough for rivers of size. There are innumerable streams, for the island generally is well-watered. The only river of real importance is the Cauto, in Oriente Province. This is the longest and the largest river in the island. It rises in the hills north of Santiago, and winds a devious way westward for about a hundred and fifty miles, emptying at last into the Gulf of Buena Esperanza, north of the city of Manzanillo. It is navigable for small boats, according to the stage of the water, from seventy-five to a hundred miles from its mouth. Numerous smaller streams flow to the coast on both north and south. Some, that are really estuaries, are called rivers. Very few of them serve any commercial purposes. There are a few water areas called lakes, but they are really little other than ponds. On the south coast, directly opposite Matanzas, lies a vast swamp known as the Cienega de Zapata. It occupies an area of about seventy-five miles in length and about thirty miles in width, almost a dead flat, and practically at sea-level. Here and there are open spaces of water or clusters of trees, but most of it is bog and quagmire and dense mangrove thickets. Along the coast are numerous harbors, large and small, that are or, by dredging, could be made available for commercial purposes. Among these, on the north coast, from west to east, are Bahia Honda, Mariel, Havana, Matanzas, Nuevitas, Nipe Bay, and Baracoa. On the south, from east to west, are Guantanamo, Santiago, Manzanillo, Cienfuegos, and Batabano. At all of these, there are now cities or towns with trade either by steamers or small sailing vessels. Among the interesting physical curiosities of the island are the numerous "disappearing rivers." Doubtless the action of water on limestone has left, in many places, underground chambers and tunnels into which the streams have found an opening and in which they disappear, perhaps to emerge again and perhaps to find their way to the sea without reappearance. This seems to explain numerous fresh-water springs among the keys and off-shore. The Rio San Antonio quite disappears near San Antonio de los Banos. Near Guantanamo, a cascade drops three hundred feet into a cavern and reappears a short distance away. Such disappearing rivers are not unknown elsewhere but Cuba has several of them.

The Census Report of 1907, prepared under American auspices, states that "the climate of Cuba is tropical and insular. There are no extremes of heat, and there is no cold weather." This is quite true if the records of a thermometer are the standard; quite untrue if measured by the sensations of the human body. It is true that, in Havana, for instance, the thermometer seldom exceeds 90° in the hottest months, and rarely if ever goes below 50° in the coldest. But a day with the thermometer anywhere in the 80s may seem to a northern body very hot, and a day with the thermometer in the 50s is cold for anyone, whether a native or a visitor. There is doubtless a physical reason for the fact that a hot day in the north seems hotter than the same temperature in the south, while a day that seems, in the north, only pleasantly cool, seems bitterly cold in the tropics. When the thermometer drops below 60° in Havana, the coachmen blanket their horses, the people put on all the clothes they have, and all visitors who are at all sensitive to low temperature go about shivering. Steam heat and furnaces are unknown, and fireplaces are a rarity. Yet, in general, the variations are not wide, either from day to day or when measured by seasons. The extremes are the infrequent exceptions. Nor is there wide difference between day and night. Taking the island as a whole, the average mean temperature for July, the hottest month, is about 82°, and for January, the coolest month, about 71°. The mean for the year is about 77°, as compared with 52° for New York, 48° for Chicago, 62° for Los Angeles, and 68° for New Orleans. There are places that, by reason of exposure to prevailing winds, or distance from the coast, are hotter or cooler than other places. Havana is one of the cool spots, that is, relatively cool. But no one goes there in search of cold. The yearly range in Havana, from maximum to minimum, rarely if ever exceeds fifty degrees, and is usually somewhat below that, while the range in New York, Chicago, and St. Louis is usually from one hundred to one hundred and twenty-five degrees. The particular cause of discomfort for those unused to it, is the humidity that prevails throughout the greater part of the year. The worst season for this, however, is the mid-year months when few people visit the island. The winter months, locally known as the "*invierno*," a term to be associated with our word "vernal" and not with "infernal," are almost invariably delightful, bringing to northern systems a pleasurable physical laziness that is attended by a mental indifference to, or satisfaction with, the sensation.

The rainfall varies so widely in different parts of the island, and from year to year, that exact information is difficult. Taken as a whole, it is little if at all greater than it is in most places in the United States. We have our arid spots, like El Paso, Fresno, Boise, Phoenix, and Winnemucca, where only a few inches fall in a year, just as Cuba has a few places where the fall may reach sixty-five or seventy inches in a year. But the average fall in Havana, Matanzas, Cienfuegos, and Santiago, is little if any greater than in Boston, New York, or Washington. A difference appears in the fact that about three-quarters of Cuba's precipitation comes between the first of May and the first of October. But the term "wet season" does not mean that it rains all the time, or every day, any more than the term "dry season" means that during those months it does not rain at all. At times during the winter, or dry season, there come storms that are due to unusual cold in the United States. These are known in Cuba, as they are in Texas, as "northers." High winds sweep furiously across the Gulf of Mexico, piling up huge seas on the Cuban coast, and bringing what, in the island, is the substitute for cold weather, usually attended by rain and sometimes by a torrent of it. The prevailing wind in Cuba is the northeast trade-wind. In summer when the sun is directly overhead this wind is nearly east, while in winter it is northeast. The proper way to avoid such discomfort as attends humidity accompanying a thermometer in the 80s, is to avoid haste in movement, to saunter instead of hurrying, to ride instead of walking, to eat and drink in moderation, and where-ever possible, to keep in the shade. Many of those who eat heartily and hurry always, will, after a few days, be quite sure that they have yellow fever or some other tropical disorder, but will be entirely mistaken about it. Modern sanitation in Cuba has made yellow fever a remote possibility, and the drinking water in Havana is as pure as any in the world.

Most of the official descriptions of the flora of Cuba appear to be copied from Robert T. Hill's book, published in 1898. As nothing better is available, it may be used here. He says: "The surface of the island is clad in a voluptuous floral mantle, which, from its abundance and beauty, first caused Cuba to be designated the Pearl of the Antilles. In addition to those introduced from abroad, over 3,350 native plants have been catalogued. The flora includes nearly all characteristic forms of the other West Indies, the southern part of Florida, and the Central American seaboard. Nearly all the large trees of the Mexican *Tierra Caliente*, so remarkable for their size, foliage, and fragrance, reappear in western Cuba. Numerous species of palm, including the famous royal palm, occur, while the pine trees, elsewhere characteristic of the temperate zone and the high altitudes of the tropics, are found associated with palms and mahoganies in the province of Pinar del Rio and the Isle of Pines, both of which take their name from this tree. Among other woods are the lignum-vitae, granadilla, the coco-wood, and the *Cedrela Odorata* (fragrant cedar) which is used for cigar boxes and the lining of cabinet work."

In quoting the number of native plants, Mr. Hill uses a report somewhat antiquated. Later estimates place the number as between five and six thousand. Flowers are abundant, flowers on vines, plants, shrubs, and trees, tall stalks with massive heads, and dainty little blossoms by the wayside. Brilliant flowering trees are planted to line the roadsides. Among all the tree-growths, the royal palm is notable. Scoffers have likened it to "a feather duster stood on end," but it is the prominent feature in most of Cuba's landscape, and it serves many purposes other than that of mere decoration. From its stem the Cuban peasant builds his little cottage which he roofs with its leaves. Medicinal qualities are claimed for its roots. From different parts of the tree, a wide variety of useful articles is made, plates, buckets, basins, and even a kettle in which water may be boiled. The huge clusters of seeds are excellent food for animals, and I have heard it said, though without proper confirmation, that "a royal palm will keep a hog." Almost invariably, its presence indicates a rich soil, as it rarely grows in areas of poor land. The forest area of the island is not known with exactness, and is variously estimated at from about six thousand square miles to about sixteen thousand. The difference probably represents the opinion of individual investigators as to what is forest. About one-third of the total is reported as in Oriente, another third in Camaguey, and the remainder scattered through the four remaining provinces. A part of it is "public land," that is, owned by the central government, but a greater part is of private ownership under old Spanish grants. Much of it is dense jungle through which a way can be made only by hacking, almost foot by foot. A good deal of it has already been cut over for its most valuable timber. Most of the woods bear names entirely unfamiliar to us. Some are used as cabinet woods, and some for tanning, for oils, dyes, gums, or fibres.

Cuba has few four-footed native wild animals. There are rabbits, but their nativity is not quite certain. There are deer, but it is known that their ancestors were brought from some other country. There are wild dogs, wild cats, and wild pigs, but all are only domestic animals run wild.

Perhaps the only animal of the kind known to be native is the *jutia*, sometimes spelled, as pronounced, *hutia*. Some observers have referred to it as a rat, but it climbs trees and grows to the size of a woodchuck, or groundhog. It is sometimes eaten and is said to be quite palatable. Reptiles are fairly common, but none of them is dangerous. The best known is the *maja*, a snake that grows to a length, sometimes, of twelve or fifteen feet. The country people not infrequently make of it a kind of house pet. When that is done, the reptile often makes its home in the cottage thatch, living on birds and mice. They are dull and sluggish in motion. While visiting a sugar plantation a few years ago one of the hands asked if I should be interested by their *maja*. He dipped his hand into a nearby water-barrel in the bottom of which two of them were closely coiled. He dragged out one of perhaps ten or twelve feet in length and four or five inches in diameter, handling it as he would the same length of hawser. He hung it over the limb of a tree so that I could have a good chance for a picture of it. The thing squirmed slowly to the ground and crawled sluggishly away to the place from which it had been taken. Of bird-life there is a large representation, both native and migratory. Among them are some fifty species of "waders." In some parts of the island, the very unpleasant land-crab, about the size of a soup-plate, seems to exist in millions, although thousands is probably nearer the actual. The American soldiers made their acquaintance in large numbers at the time of the Santiago campaign. They are not a proper article of food. They have a salt-water relative that is most excellent eating, as is also the lobster *(langosta)* of Cuban waters. In the swamp known as the Cienega de Zapata are both alligators and crocodiles, some of them of quite imposing dimensions.

The insect life of the island is extensive. From personal experience, particularly behind the search-light of an automobile that drew them in swarms, I, should say that the island would be a rich field for the entomologist. There are mosquitos, gnats, beetles, moths, butterflies, spiders, and scorpions. The bites of some of the spiders and the stings of the scorpions are, of course, uncomfortable, but they are neither fatal nor dangerous. With the exception of an occasional mosquito, and a perhaps more than occasional flea, the visitor to cities only is likely to encounter few of the members of these branches of Cuban zoology. There is one of the beetle family, however, that is extremely interesting. That is the *cucullo*, which Mr. Hazard, in his book on Cuba, calls a "bright peripatetic candle-bearer, by whose brilliant light one can not only walk, but even read." They are really a kind of glorified firefly, much larger than ours, and with a much more brilliant light. I do not know their candle-power, but Mr. Hazard exaggerates little if at all in the matter of their brilliancy.

While those referred to in the foregoing are the most notable features in this particular part of the Cuban field, there are others, though of perhaps less importance, to which reference might be made. Among them would be the sponge fisheries of the coast in the neighborhood of Batabano, and the numerous mineral springs, some of them really having, and others supposed to have, remarkable curative qualities. A half century or so ago, a number of places not far from Havana were resorts to which rich and poor went to drink or to bathe in springs hot or cold or sulphurous or otherwise, for their healing. Among these were the baths at San Diego, near the Organ Mountains in Pinar del Rio; Santa Rita, near Guanabacoa in Havana Province; others near Marianao, on the outskirts of the city; and San Antonio, also in Havana Province. Most of these places now appear to have lost their popularity if not their medicinal virtues. Some, like those at Madruga, not far from Havana, still have a considerable patronage. Something may also be said of earthquakes and hurricanes. The former occur, on a small scale, more or less frequently in Oriente, and much less frequently and of less severity in Havana. The latter come from time to time to work disaster to Cuban industries and, sometimes but not frequently, to cause loss of life and the destruction of buildings. They rarely occur except in the late summer and the autumn.

Nearly a hundred years ago, Alexander Humboldt, a traveller and a scientist, wrote thus of the island of Cuba: "Notwithstanding the absence of deep rivers and the unequal fertility of the soil, the island of Cuba presents on every hand a most varied and agreeable country from its undulating character, its ever-springing verdure, and the variety of its vegetable formations."

IV

THE OLD HAVANA

Among the many pictures, stored away in the album of my memory, there are two that stand out more vividly than any others. The subjects are separated by half the world's circumference. One is the sunsets at Jolo, in the southern Philippines. There the sun sank into the western sea in a blaze of cloud-glory, between the low-lying islands on either hand with the rich green of their foliage turned to purple shadows. The other is the sunrise at Havana, seen from the deck of a steamer in the harbor. The long, soft shadows and the mellow light fell on the blue and gray and green of the buildings of the city, and on the red-tiled roofs, with the hills for a background in one-half of the picture, and the gleaming water of the gulf in the background of the other half. I had seen the long stretch of the southern coast of the island, from Cape Antonio to Cape Maisi, while on an excursion with a part of the army of occupation sent to Porto Rico in the summer of 1898, and had set foot on Cuban soil at Daiquiri, but Havana in the morning light, on January 2, 1899, was my first real Cuban experience. It remains an ineffaceable memory. Of my surroundings and experiences aside from that, I have no distinct recollection. All was submerged by that one picture, and quickly buried by the activities into which I was immediately plunged. I do not recall the length of time we were held on board for medical inspection, nor whether the customs inspection was on board or ashore. I recall the trip from the ship to the wharf, in one of the little sailboats then used for the purpose, rather because of later experiences than because of the first one. I have no purpose here to write a history of those busy days, filled as they were with absorbing interest, with much that was pathetic and not a little that was amusing. I have seen that morning picture many times since, but never less beautiful, never less impressive. Nowadays, it is lost to most travellers because the crossing from Key West is made in the daytime, the boat reaching Havana in the late-afternoon. Sometimes there is a partial compensation in the sunset picture, but I have never seen that when it really rivalled the picture at the beginning of the day.

The visitor to Cuba, unfamiliar with the island, should take it leisurely. It is not a place through which the tourist may rush, guide book in hand, making snapshots with a camera, and checking off places of interest as they are visited. Picturesqueness and quaintness are not at all lacking, but there are no noble cathedrals, no vast museums of art and antiquity, no snow-clad mountains. There is a charm of light and shade and color that is to be absorbed slowly rather than swallowed at a single gulp. It is emphatically a place in which to dawdle. Let those who are obliged to do so, work and hurry; the visitor and the traveller should take it without haste. It is far better to see Havana and its vicinity slowly and enjoyably, and look at pictures of the rest of the country, than it is to rush through the island merely for the sake of doing so. In his essay on *The Moral of Landscape,* Mr. Ruskin said that "all travelling becomes dull in exact proportion to its rapidity." Nowhere is that more true than it is in Cuba. There is very little in all the island that cannot be seen in Havana and its immediate vicinity. It is well to see the other places if one has ample time, but they should not be seen at the expense of a proper enjoyment of Havana and its neighborhood. In Havana are buildings as old and buildings as beautiful as any in the island. In its vicinity are sugar plantations, tobacco fields, pineapples, cocoanuts, mangoes, royal palms, ceibas, peasants' homes, typical towns and villages, all the life of the people in the city and country. The common American desire to "see it all" in a few days, is fatal to the greatest enjoyment, and productive mainly of physical fatigue and mental confusion. It is the misfortune of most travellers that they carry with them only the vaguest of ideas of what they want to see. They have heard of Cuba, of Havana, the Morro, the Prado, of a sunny island in the midst of a sapphire sea. While it is true that almost everything in Cuba is worth seeing, it is best to acquire, before going, some idea of the exhibition. That saves time and many steps. The old city wall, La Fuerza, and La Punta, are mere piles of masonry, more or less dull and uninteresting unless one knows something of their history. The manners and customs of any country become increasingly interesting if one knows something about them, the reason for them.

It is only a short trip to the Castillo del Principe, the fortress that crowns the hill to the west of the city. From that height, the city and the harbor are seen below, to the eastward. Across the bay, on the heights at the entrance, are the frowning walls of Morro Castle surmounted by the towering light-house, and the no less grim walls of La Cabaña. The bay itself is a sprawling, shapeless body of water with a narrow neck connecting it with the Florida Straits. Into the western side of the bay the city thrusts itself in a shape that, on a large map, suggests more than anything else the head and neck of an over-fed bulldog. Into this bay, in 1508, came Sebastian Ocampo, said to be the first white man to visit the spot. He entered for the purpose of careening his little vessels in order to remove the barnacles and accumulated weed-growth. It is possible that the spot was discovered earlier, but there is no record of the discovery if such was made. Ocampo gave it the name of Puerto de Carenas. The next record is of its occupation, in 1519. Four years earlier, Diego Velasquez had left a little colony near what is now called Batabano, on the south coast. He gave the place the name of San Cristobal de la Habana, in memory of the illustrious navigator and discoverer. Habana, or Havana, is a term of aboriginal origin. It proved to be an uncomfortable place of residence, and in 1519 the people moved across the island to the Puerto de Carenas, taking with them the name given to the earlier settlement, and substituting it for the name given by Ocampo. After a time, all was dropped except the present title, Habana, or more commonly by English-speaking people, Havana. It was not much of a place for a number of years, but in 1538 it was sacked and burned by a French pirate, one of the many, of different nations, who carried on a very lively buccaneering business in those and in later years in West Indian waters. Hernando de Soto was then governor of the island, with headquarters at the then capital city, Santiago de Cuba. He proceeded at once to the scene of destruction. On his arrival, he ordered the erection of a fortress. Some of the work then done still remains in the old structure near the Palace, at the foot of Calle O'Reilly, known as La Fuerza. A few years before this time, Hernan Cortes had conquered Mexico, then called New Spain, and a business between Old Spain and New Spain soon developed. The harbor of Havana made a convenient halting-place on the voyages between the two, and the settlement assumed a steadily increasing importance. A new governor, Gonzales Perez de Angulo, who arrived in 1549, decided to make it his place of residence. The year 1552 is generally given as the time of the creation of Havana as the capital city. It was at that time made the residence city of the Governors, by their own choice, but it was not officially established as the capital until 1589. The fortress erected by order of de Soto proved somewhat ineffective. In 1554, another French marauder attacked and destroyed the town. The principal industry of those early days was cattle-raising, a considerable market being developed for export to Mexico, and for the supply of vessels that entered the harbor for food and water.

The continuance of incursions by pirates made necessary some further provision for the defence of the city. In 1589, La Fuerza was enlarged and strengthened, and the construction of Morro Castle was begun. To this work was added La Punta, the little fortress on the western shore of the entrance, at the point of the angle now formed by the Prado and the Malecon. These ancient structures, of practically no value whatever in modern warfare, are now among the most picturesque points of interest in the neighborhood. Another, in the same class, of which only a little now remains, is of a later time. This is the old city wall, the construction of which was begun in 1671. Following the simile of the bull-dog's head, a tract of land, formerly known as the Arsenal yard, and now the central railway station, lies tucked away immediately under the animal's jaw. From there to a point on the north shore, near La Punta, in a slightly curving line, a high wall was erected for the purpose of defence on the western or landward side. The old city lay entirely in the area defined by this western wall and the shore of the harbor. At intervals, gates afforded exit to the country beyond, heavy gates that could be closed to exclude any possible attacking party. The fortifications erected from time to time were supposed to afford a system of effective defence for the city. They are now little else than picturesque features in the landscape, points of interest for visitors. Taking the chain in its order, El Morro stands on the point on the eastern side of the entrance to the harbor. Just beyond it is La Cabaña. About a half a mile to the east of this was the stone fort on the hill of San Diego. Three miles east of the Morro, on the shore at Cojimar, is a small and somewhat ancient fortification. This group constituted the defence system on the east. At the head of the bay, on an elevation a little to the south of the city, stands El Castillo de Atares, begun in 1763, immediately after the capture and occupation of the city by the British. This is supposed to protect the city on the south, as Castillo del Principe is supposed to defend it on the west. This stands on a hill on the western outskirts, a somewhat extensive structure, begun in 1774 and completed about twenty years later. A little further to the west, at the mouth of the Almendares river, stands a little fort, or tower, called Chorrera, serving as a western outpost as Cojimar serves as an eastern outpost. Both were erected about the year 1650. On the shore generally north of Principe was the Santa Clara battery, and between that and La Punta, at the foot of the Calzada de Belascoain, stood the Queen's battery. From any modern point of view, the system is little more than military junk, better fitted for its present use as barracks, asylums, and prisons than for military defence. But it is all highly picturesque.

In the beginning, most of the buildings of the city were doubtless of wood, with palm-thatched roofs. In time, these gave place to rows of abutting stone buildings with tiled roofs. Most of them were of one story, some were of two stories, and a few "palaces" had three. The city within the wall is today very much as it was a century and more ago. Its streets run, generally but not accurately, at right angles, one set almost due east and west, from the harbor front to the line of the old wall, and the other set runs southward from the shore of the entrance channel to the shore of the inner harbor. Several of these streets are practically continuous from north to south or from east to west. But most of them are rather passage-ways than streets. The houses come to their very edges, except for a narrow strip hardly to be classed as a sidewalk, originally left, presumably, only for the purpose of preventing the scraping of the front of the building by the wheels of passing carts and carriages. It is a somewhat inconvenient system nowadays, but one gets quite used to it after a little, threads the narrow walk a part of his way, takes to the street the rest of the way, and steps aside to avoid passing vehicles quite as did the carriageless in the old days. One excellent way to avoid the trouble is to take a carriage and let the other fellow step aside. Riding in the *coche* is still one of the cheapest forms of convenience and entertainment in the city, excepting the afternoon drive around the Prado and the Malecon. That is not cheap. We used to pay a dollar an hour. My last experience cost me three times that.

Much of the old city is now devoted to business purposes, wholesale, retail, and professional. But there are also residences, old churches, and old public buildings. On the immediate water-front, and for many years used as the custom house, stands the old Franciscan convent, erected during the last quarter of the 16th Century. It is a somewhat imposing pile, dominated by a high tower. I have not visited it for a number of years and do not know if its interior is available for visitors without some special introduction, but there is much worth seeing inside its walls, the flying buttresses of the super-structure, some old and interesting frescoes, and a system of dome construction that is quite remarkable. To the latter, my attention was first called by General Ludlow, a distinguished engineer officer of the United States Army, then acting as governor of the city. To him belongs, although it is very rarely given, the credit for the cleansing of Havana during the First Intervention. He frequently visited the old convent just to see and study that interior dome construction. Immediately behind the Palace is the old convent of the Dominicans, less imposing but of about the same period as the Franciscan structure. It is now used as a high-school building. The

Cathedral, a block to the northward of the Dominican convent building, is of a much later date, having been begun as recently as 1742. It was originally the convent of the Jesuits, but became the Cathedral in 1789. Many have believed, on what seems to be acceptable evidence, that here for more than a hundred years rested the bones of Christopher Columbus. He died in Valladolid in 1506, and was buried there. His remains were removed to the Carthusian Monastery, in Seville, in 1513. From there they are said to have been taken, in 1536, to the city of Santo Domingo, where they remained until 1796, when they were brought to Havana and placed in a niche in the walls of the old Cathedral, there to remain until they were taken back to Spain in 1898. There is still an active dispute as to whether the bones removed from Santo Domingo to Havana were or were not those of Columbus. At all events, the urn supposed to contain them was in this building for a hundred years, below a marble slab showing a carving of the voyager holding a globe, with a finger pointing to the Caribbean. Beneath this was a legend that has been thus translated:

OH! REST THOU, IMAGE OF THE GREAT COLON,
THOUSAND CENTURIES REMAIN, GUARDED IN THE URN,
AND IN THE REMEMBRANCE OF OUR NATION.

In this neighborhood, to the east of the Plaza de Armas, on which the Palace fronts, is a structure known as *El Templete*. It has the appearance of the portico of an unfinished building, but it is a finished memorial, erected in 1828. The tradition is that on this spot there stood, in 1519, an old ceiba tree under which the newly arrived settlers celebrated their first mass. The yellow Palace, for many years the official headquarters and the residence of successive Governors-General, stands opposite, and speaks for itself. In this building, somewhat devoid of architectural merit, much of Cuba's history, for the last three-quarters of a century, has been written. The best time to see all this and much more that is to be seen, is the early morning, before the wheels begin to go around. The lights and shadows are then the best, and the streets are quieter and less crowded. The different points of interest are easily located by the various guide books obtainable, and the distances are not great. A cup of *cafe con leche* should precede the excursion. If one feels lazy, as one is quite apt to feel in the tropics and the sub-tropics, fairly comfortable open carriages are at all times available. With them, of course, a greater area can be covered and more places seen, though perhaps seen less satisfactorily. There is much to be seen in the early morning that is best seen in those hours, and much that is not seen later in the day. In all cities there is an early morning life and Havana is no exception. I confess to only a limited personal knowledge of it, but I have seen enough of it, and heard enough about it, to know that the waking-up of cities, including Havana, is an interesting process. I have, at least, had enough personal experience to be sure that the early morning air is delicious, the best of the day. I am not speaking of the unholy hours preceding daybreak, but of six to eight o'clock, which for those of us who are inclined to long evenings is also the best time to be in bed. The early morning church bells are a disturbance to which visitors do not readily adjust their morning naps. Mr. Samuel Hazard, who visited Cuba about the year 1870, and wrote quite entertainingly about it, left the following description of his experience in Havana:

"Hardly has the day begun to break when the newly arrived traveller is startled from his delightful morning doze by the alarming sound of bells ringing from every part of the town. Without any particular concert of action, and with very different sounds, they ring out on the still morning air, as though for a general conflagration, and the unfortunate traveller rushes frantically from his bed to inquire if there is any hope of safety from the flames which he imagines, from the noise made, must threaten the whole town. Imagine, O reader! in thy native town, every square with its church, every church with its tower, or maybe two or three of them, and in each particular tower a half-dozen large bells, no two of which sound alike; place the bell-ropes in the hands of some frantic man who pulls away, first with one hand and then the other, and you will get a very faint idea of your first awakening in Havana. Without apparent rhyme or reason, ding, dong, ding they go, every bell-ringer at each different church striving to see how much noise he can make, under the plea of bringing the faithful to their prayers at the early morning mass."

The only conceivable advantage of these early bells is the fact that they turn out many a traveller at the hour when Havana is really at its best. Yet, as I read the descriptive tales left by those who wrote forty, fifty, and sixty years ago, I am struck by the fact, that, after all, the old Havana has changed but little. There are trolley lines, electric lights, and a few other so-called modern improvements, but there is still much of the old custom, the old atmosphere. The old wall, with its soldier-guarded gates, is gone, and there are a few modern buildings, but only a few, for which fact I always feel thankful, but the old city is much what it was when Mr. Ballou, and Mr. Dana, and Mr. Kimball, and numerous others wrote about it soon after 1850, and when Mr. Hazard wrote about it in 1870. The automobile is there now in large numbers, in place of the old volante, and there are asphalted streets in place of cobble-stones. The band plays in the evening in the Parque Central or at the Glorieta, instead of in the Plaza de Armas, but the band plays. The restaurants are still a prominent feature in Havana life, as they were then. The ladies wear hats instead of *mantillas*, but they buy hats on Calle Obispo just as and where their mothers and grandmothers bought *mantillas*. Bull-fighting is gone, presumably forever, but crowds flock to the baseball grounds. The midday suspension of business continues, generally, and the afternoon parade, on foot and in carriages, remains one of the important functions of the day. There are many who know Havana, and love it, who pray diligently that it may be many years before the city is Americanized as, for instance, New Orleans has been.

Most of the life of the city, as it is seen by most visitors, is outside the old city, and probably few know that any distinction is made, yet the line is drawn with fair clearness. There is a different appearance in both streets and buildings. While there are shops on San Rafael and Galiano and elsewhere, the principal shopping district is in the old city, with Calle Obispo as its centre. They have tried officially, to change the name of the street, but the old familiar name sticks and seems likely to stick for a long time yet. Far be it from a mere man to attempt analysis or description of such a place. He might tell another mere man where to buy a hat, a pair of shoes, or eyeglasses, or a necktie, or where to find a lawyer, but the finer points of shopping, there or elsewhere, are not properly for any masculine description. The ladies may be trusted to learn for themselves, and very quickly, all that they need or want to know about that phase of Havana's commerce. I am leaving much to the guide books that can afford space for all necessary information about churches, statues, and other objects of interest for visitors. Havana's retail merchants have their own way of trading, much as they do in many foreign countries, and in not a few stores in our own country. Prices are usually a question of the customer's ability to match the commercial shrewdness of the dealer. Much of the trade of visitors is now confined to the purchase of such articles as may be immediately needed and to a few souvenirs. One of the charms of the place is the cheap transportation. If you are tired, or in a hurry, there is always a coach near at hand that will take you where you wish to go, for a peseta, or a quarter, if within certain officially prescribed bounds. If you desire to go beyond those bounds, make a bargain with your driver or be prepared for trouble. Down in the old city are to be found several restaurants that are well worth visiting, for those who want good food. I shall not advertise the particular places, but they are well known. As the early morning is the best time to see the old city, the forenoon is the best time for shopping. Such an expedition may well be followed by the *almuerzo*, the midday breakfast or lunch, whichever one sees fit to call it, at one of these restaurants. After that, it is well to enjoy a midday *siesta*, in preparation for the afternoon function on the Prado and the Malecon.

V

THE NEW HAVANA

The new Havana, the city outside the old wall, is about as old as Chicago but not nearly as tall. There is no reason why it should be. Here are wide streets and broad avenues, and real sidewalks, some of them about as wide as the entire street in the old city. About 1830, the region beyond the wall was held largely by Spaniards to whom grants of land had been made for one reason or another. These tracts were plantations, pastures, or unimproved lands, according to the fancy of the proprietor who usually lived in the city and enjoyed himself after the manner of his kind. Here and there, a straggling village of palm-leaf huts sprang up. The roads were rough tracks. To Governor-General Tacon seems due much of the credit for the improvement beyond the walls. During his somewhat iron-handed rule several notable buildings were erected, some of them by his authority. The most notable feature of the district is the renowned Prado, a broad boulevard with a park between two drive-ways, running from the water-front, at the entrance to the harbor, southward for about a mile. A few years ago, rows of trees shaded the central parkway, but they were almost entirely wrecked by the hurricanes in 1906 and 1910.

A half mile or so from its northern end, the Prado runs along the west side of the Parque Central, the most notable of the numerous little squares of walks and trees and flowers. A block or two further on is a little park with an excellent statue, known as La India. Opposite that is another really beautiful park, from the western side of which runs a broad street that leads to the Paseo de Carlos Tercero, formerly the Paseo de Tacon, one of the monuments left to his own memory by one of Cuba's most noted Spanish rulers. The Paseo runs westward to El Castillo del Principe, originally a fortress but now a penitentiary. The Prado stops just beyond the companion parks, La India and Colon. These originally formed the Campo de Marte, laid out by General Tacon and, in his time, used as a military parade ground. In a way, the Parque Central is the centre of the city. It is almost that, geographically, and perhaps quite that, socially. In its immediate vicinity are some of the leading hotels and the principal theatres. One of the latter, facing the park on its western side, across the Prado, is now known as the Nacional. Formerly it was the Tacon, a monument to that notable man. There is quite a story about that structure. It is somewhat too long for inclusion here, but it seems worth telling. The following is an abridgment of the tale as it is told in Mr. Ballou's *History of Cuba*, published in 1854. Tacon was the Governor of the island from 1834 to 1838. At that time, a certain man named Marti was eminent in the smuggling and piracy business, an industry in which many others were engaged. But Marti seems to have stood at the top of his profession, a man of skill and daring and evidently well supplied with brains. Tacon's efforts to capture him, or to break up his business, were entirely unsuccessful, and a large reward was offered for his body, alive or dead. Mr. Ballou tells the story in somewhat dramatic manner:

"It was a dark, cloudy night in Havana, a few months after the announcement of the reward, when two sentinels were pacing backward and forward before the main entrance to the Governor's palace. A little before midnight, a man was watching them from behind a statue in the park, and after observing that the sentinels paced their brief walk so as to meet each other, and then turned their backs as they separated, leaving a brief moment in the interval when the eyes of both were turned away from the entrance, seemed to calculate upon passing them unobserved. It was an exceedingly delicate manoeuvre, and required great care and dexterity to effect it; but, at last, it was adroitly done, and the stranger sprang lightly through the entrance, secreting himself behind one of the pillars of the inner court. The sentinels paced on undisturbed. The figure which had thus stealthily effected an entrance, now sought the broad stairs that led to the Governor's suite, with a confidence that evinced a perfect knowledge of the place. A second guard-post was to be passed at the head of the stairs; but, assuming an air of authority, the stranger offered a cold military salute and passed forward, as though there was not the most distant question of his right to do so; and thus avoiding all suspicion in the guard's mind, he boldly entered the Governor's reception room unchallenged, and closed the door behind him."

In his office, alone, the stranger found Tacon, who was naturally surprised at the appearance of an unannounced caller. He demanded to know who the visitor was, but a direct answer was evaded. After referring to the matter of the reward offered for the discovery of Marti, and the pledge of immunity to the discoverer, the caller demanded and obtained a verbal endorsement of the promise of immunity, under the Governor's word of honor, whatever might be the circumstances of his revelation. He then announced himself as the much-sought pirate and smuggler, Marti. Tacon was somewhat astounded, but he kept his word. Marti was held overnight, but "on the following day," the Ballou account proceeds, "one of the men-of-war that lay idly beneath the guns of Morro Castle suddenly became the scene of the utmost activity, and, before noon, had weighed her anchor, and was standing out into the gulf stream. Marti the smuggler was on board as her pilot; and faithfully did he guide the ship on the discharge of his treacherous business, revealing every haunt of the rovers, exposing their most valuable depots; and many a smuggling craft was taken and destroyed. The amount of money and property thus secured was very great." The contemptible job of betraying his former companions and followers being successfully accomplished, Marti returned with the ships, and claimed his reward from Tacon. The General, according to his word of honor, gave Marti a full and unconditional pardon for all his past offences, and an order on the treasury for the amount of the reward offered. The latter was declined but, in lieu of the sum, Marti asked for and obtained a monopoly of the right to sell fish in Havana. He offered to build, at his own expense, a public market of stone, that should, after a specified term of years, revert to the government, "with all right and the title to the fishery." This struck Tacon as a good business proposition; he saved to his treasury the important sum of the reward and, after a time, the city would own a valuable fish-market. He agreed to the plan. Marti thereupon went into the fish business, made huge profits, and became, so the story goes, the richest man in the island. After a time, being burdened with wealth, he looked about for means of increasing his income. So he asked for and obtained a monopoly of the theatre business in Havana, promising to build one of the largest and finest theatres in the world. The result of the enterprise was the present Nacional theatre, for many years regarded as second only to the Grand theatre in Milan. But it was named the Tacon. Its special attraction was internal; its exterior was far from imposing. It has recently been considerably glorified. Having thus halted for the story of the theatre, we may return to the Prado on which it fronts. Here, Havana society used to gather every afternoon to drive, walk, and talk. The afternoon *paseo* was and still is the great event of the day, the great social function of the city. At the time of my first visit, in 1899, there was no Malecon drive along the shore to the westward. That enterprise was begun during the First Intervention, and continued by succeeding administrations. In the earlier days, the route for driving was down the east side of the Prado, between the Parque Central and the *Carcel*, and up the west side, around and around, up and down, with bows and smiles to acquaintances met or passed, and, probably, gossip about the strangers. Many horsemen appeared in the procession, and the central promenade was thronged with those who walked, either because they preferred to or because they could not afford to ride around and around. In the Parque Central were other walkers, chatting groups, and lookers-on. Some days the band played. Then the Prado was extended to the water-front; the *glorieta* was erected; and that became another centre for chatterers and watchers. The building of the Malecon extended the range of the driveway. This afternoon function is an old established institution and a good one. It may not compare favorably with the drive in some of our parks in this country, but it is the best substitute possible in Havana. Indulgence in ices, cooling drinks, chocolate, or other refections, during this daily ceremony, is fairly common but by no means a general practice. The afternoon tea habit has not yet seized upon Havana. The ices are almost invariably excellent. Some of them are prepared from native fruit flavors that are quite unknown here. The *guanabana* ice is particularly to be recommended. All such matters are quite individual, but a decoction called *chocolate Espanol* is also to be recommended. It is served hot, too thick to drink, and is to be taken with a spoon, to the accompaniment of cake. It is highly nourishing as well as palatable. There is a wide variety of "soft drinks," made with oranges, limes, or other fruits, and the *orchata*, made from almonds, and the products of American soda fountains, but there is little use of the high-ball or the cocktail except by Americans.

The Cubans are an exceedingly temperate people. Wine is used by all classes, and *aguadiente*, the native rum, is consumed in considerable quantity, but the Cuban rarely drinks to excess. I recall an experience during the earlier years. I was asked to write a series of articles on the use of intoxicants in the island, for a temperance publication in this country. My first article so offended the publishers that they declined to print it, and cancelled the order for the rest of the series. It was perhaps somewhat improper, but in that article I summed up the situation by stating that "the temperance question in Cuba is only a question of how soon we succeed in converting them into a nation of drunkards." Beer is used, both imported and of local manufacture. Gin, brandy, and anisette, cordials and liqueurs are all used to some but moderate extent, but intoxication is quite rare. One fluid extract I particularly recommend, that is the milk of the cocoanut, the green nut. Much, however, depends upon the cocoanut. Properly ripened, the "milk" is delicious, cooling and wholesome, more so perhaps on a country journey than in the city. The nut not fully ripened gives the milk, or what is locally called the "water," an unpleasant, woody taste. I have experimented with it in different parts of the world, in the Philippines, Ceylon, and elsewhere, and have found it wholesome and refreshing in all places.

The houses in the new Havana are, on the whole, vastly more cheerful than are the dwellings in the old city. They are of the same general architectural type, but because of the wider streets, more air and sunshine gets into them. Some of the best and most costly are along the Prado. A Cuban house interior generally impresses an American as lacking in home-like quality. Some of the best are richly adorned, but there is a certain bareness and an absence of color. As is usual with customs unlike our own, and which we are therefore prone to regard as inferior to ours, there are excellent reasons for Cuban interior decoration, or rather the lack of it. A little experience, or even a little reflection, shows clearly the impossibility of anything resembling American house decoration in such a climate as that of Cuba. Our warm colors, hangings, upholstered furniture, rugs, and much else that we regard as essential in northern latitudes, would be utterly unendurable in Cuba. There, the marble or tiled floors, the cool tones of wall and ceiling, and the furniture of wood and cane, are not only altogether fitting but as well altogether necessary. Our glass windows would only serve to increase heat and shut out air. As some barrier is necessary to keep passers, even Americans, from intrusive entrance by the windows whose bottoms are at floor level, the system of iron bars or elaborate grille work is adopted. Few Americans see much, if anything, of Cuban home life except as they see it through these barriers as they pass. It is not the custom of the country to invite promiscuous or casual acquaintances to call. It is even less the custom there than it is with us. A book about Cuba, published a few years ago, gives a somewhat extended account of what is called "home life," but it is the home life of workmen and people who do laundry work to eke out a meagre living. It is not even the life of fairly paid artisans, or of people of modest but comfortable income. It is no more a proper description of the domestic life of the island than would be a presentation of the life in the palaces of the wealthy. Such attempts at description are almost invariably a mistake, conveying, whether from purpose or from indifference to truth, a false impression. Domestic economy and household management vary in Cuba as they vary in the United States, in France, England, Japan, or Mexico. The selection of an individual home, or of several, as a basis for description, in Cuba or anywhere else, can only result in a picture badly out of drawing and quite misleading.

There are Cuban homes, as there are American homes, that are slatternly and badly managed, and there are Cuban homes that are as spick and span and as orderly in their administration as any home in this country. Their customs, as are ours, are the result of environment and tradition. To some of us, a rectangle of six or eight rocking-chairs, placed in the centre of a room, in which family and visitors sit and rock while they talk, may seem curious, but it is a custom that we may not criticize either with fairness or common decency. The same may be said of the not uncommon custom of using a part of the street floor of the house as a stable. It is an old custom, brought from Spain. But I have wandered from description to incident. I have no intention to attempt a description of Cuban home life, beyond saying that I have been a guest in costly homes in the city and in the little palm-leaf "shacks" of peasants, and have invariably found in both, and in the homes of intermediate classes, only cordial hospitality and gracious courtesy. Those who have found anything different have carried it with them in their own attitude toward their hosts. Many of us, probably most of us, in the United States, make a sort of fetich of the privacy of what we call our home life. We are encased in walls of wood or masonry, with blinds, curtains, or shades at our windows. It might be supposed that we wanted to hide, that there was something of which to be ashamed. It might at least be so interpreted by one unfamiliar with our ways. It is only, like the open domestic life in Cuba, a custom, a habit of long standing. Certainly, much of the domestic life of Cuba is open. The mistress of the house chides a servant, rebukes or comforts a child, sits with her embroidery, chaffers with an itinerant merchant or with the clerk from a store, all in plain sight and hearing of the passer-by. What everyone does, no one notices. The customs of any country are curious only to those from other countries where customs are different. Our ways of life are quite as curious to others as are their ways to us. We are quite blind to that fact chiefly because of an absurd conviction of the immense superiority of our ways. We do not stop to consider reasons for differences. A cup of coffee on an American breakfast table usually consists of about four parts coffee and one part milk or cream. Most Cubans usually reverse these percentages. There is a good reason for it. In our climate, we do not need the large open doors and windows, the high ceilings, and the full and free ventilation that make life endurable in tropical and sub-tropical countries. Their system here would be as impossible as would be our system there. Houses in Cuba like those of an American city or town would make life a miserable burden. The publicity, or semi-publicity, of Cuban home life is a necessary result of conditions. It is, naturally, more in evidence in the city proper, where the houses, abutting immediately on the street, as do most of our city houses, are built, as ours are, in solid rows. We avoid a good deal of publicity by piling our homes on top of each other, and by elevators and stair-climbing.

The location of a residence in Havana gives no special idea of the wealth or the social standing of those who occupy it. Not a few well-to-do people still live in the old city, where the streets are narrow and where business is trying to crowd out everything except itself. The home in that quarter may be in a block in which a number of buildings are residences, or it may stand with a warehouse on one side and a workshop on the other. A few people, of unquestionable social position still live in buildings in which the street floor is a store or an office. There is nothing curious about this. In many American cities, old families have clung to old homes, and not a few new families have, from one reason or another, occupied similar quarters. Such a residence may not conform to modern social ideas and standards, but there are Americans in this country, as well as Cubans and Spaniards in Havana, who can afford to ignore those standards. The same is true of many who live in the newer city, outside the old walls. There as here, business encroaches on many streets formerly strictly residential. This holds in the newer part of the city as well as in the old part. A number of streets there are, for a part of their length, quite given over to business. Even the Prado itself is the victim of commercial invasion. What was once one of the finest residences in the city, the old Aldama place fronting on the Campo de Marte, is now a cigar factory. A little beyond it is the Tacon market, occupying an entire block. Stores and shops surround it. The old avenue leading to the once fashionable Cerro, and to the only less fashionable Jesus del Monte, is now a business street. Another business street leads out of the Parque Central, alongside the former Tacon theatre. The broad Calzada de Galiano, once a fashionable residence street, is now largely commercial. While less picturesque than some parts of the old city within the walls, the most attractive part of Havana is undoubtedly the section of El Vedado, the westward extension along the shore. Here are broad streets, trees, gardens, and many beautiful and costly dwellings. This is really the modern Havana. A part of it is only a little above sea-level, and behind that strip is a hill. A few years ago, only a small number of houses were on the hillside or the hilltop. Now, it is well built over with modern houses. The architectural type is generally retained, and it is rather a pity that there should be even what variation there is. El Vedado is the region of the wealthy and the well-to-do, with a large percentage of foreigners. It has its social ways, very much as other places have, in this country, in France, Hong Kong, or Honolulu. They are not quite our ways, but they are a result of conditions, just as ours are.

On the hill, a little back of El Vedado, are two "points of interest" for visitors; the old fortress, el Castillo del Principe, and the cemetery. In the latter are some notable monuments. One is known as the Firemen's Monument. For many years, Havana has had, supplementary to its municipal organization, a volunteer firemen's corps. In various ways the latter resembles a number of military organizations in the United States. It is at once a somewhat exclusive social club and a practical force. Membership is a social distinction. If you are in Havana and see men in admirably tailored, uniforms and fire helmets, rushing in a particular direction in cabs, carriages or automobiles, you may know that they are members of the *Bomberos del Comercio* on their way to a conflagration. Most excellent real work they have done again and again in time of fire and flood. On parade, they look exceedingly dapper with their helmets, uniforms, boots and equipment, somewhat too dandified even to suggest any smoke other than that of cigars or cigarettes. But they are the "real thing in smoke-eaters" when they get to work. They have a long list of heroic deeds on their records. The monument in Colon Cemetery commemorates one of those deeds. In an extensive and dangerous fire, in May, 1890, thirty of these men lost their lives. A few years later, this beautiful and costly shaft was erected, by private subscription, as a tribute to their valor and devotion. Another shaft, perhaps no less notable, commemorates a deplorable and unpardonable event. A number of medical students, mere boys, in the University of Havana, were charged with defacing the tomb of a Spanish officer who had been killed by a Cuban in a political quarrel. At its worst, it was a boyish prank, demanding rebuke or even some mild punishment. Later evidence indicates that while there was a demonstration there was no defacement of the vault. Forty-two students were arrested as participants, tried by court-martial, and sentenced to be shot. Eight of them were shot at La Punta, at the foot of the Prado near the sea-front, and the remainder sentenced to imprisonment for life. All of these, I believe, were afterward released. The Students' Monument expresses the feeling of the Cubans in the matter, a noble memorial. There are numerous other shafts and memorials that are notable and interesting. A number of Cuba's leaders, Maximo Gomez, Calixto Garcia, and others, are buried in this cemetery.

Further on, to the southeast, are other sections of the new Havana, the districts of Cerro and Jesus del Monte. El Vedado has largely supplanted these neighborhoods as the "court end" of the city. Many of the fine old residences of forty or fifty years ago still remain, but most of them are now closely surrounded by the more modest homes of a less aristocratic group. A few gardens remain to suggest what they were in the earlier days. Still further out, in the west-and-south quarter-circle, are little towns, villages, and hamlets, typically Cuban, with here and there the more imposing estate of planter or proprietor. But, far the greater number of visitors, perhaps with greater reason, find more of charm and interest in the city itself than in the suburbs or the surrounding country. The enjoyment of unfamiliar places is altogether personal. There are many who really see nothing; they come away from a brief visit with only a confusion of vague recollections of sights and sounds, of brief inspection of buildings about which they knew nothing, of the big, yellow Palace, of this church and that, of the Morro and the harbor, of sunny days, and of late afternoons along the Prado and the Malecon. To me, Havana is losing its greatest charm through an excess of Americanization, slowly but steadily taking from the place much of the individuality that made it most attractive. It will be a long time before that is entirely lost, but five-story office buildings, automobiles in the afternoon parade, steaks or ham and eggs at an eight or nine o'clock breakfast, and all kinds of indescribable hats in place of dainty and graceful *mantillas*, seem to me a detraction, like bay-windows and porticos added to an old colonial mansion.

VI

AROUND THE ISLAND

A hundred years ago, the Cubans travelled from place to place about the island, just as our ancestors did in this country, by water and over rough trails few of which could, with any approach to correctness, be described as roads. It was not until about a hundred years ago that we, in this country, began to build anything even remotely resembling a modern highway. Our towns and cities were on the seaboard or on the banks of rivers navigable for vessels of size sufficient for their purposes. Commodities carried to or brought from places not so located were dragged in stoutly built wagons over routes the best of which was worse than the worst to be found anywhere today. Because real road-making in Cuba is quite a modern institution, an enterprise to which, in their phrase, the Spanish Government did not "dedicate" itself, the Cuban wagons and carts of today are chiefly those of the older time. They are heavy, cumbrous affairs with large wheels, a diameter necessitated by the deep ruts through which a passage was made. A smaller wheel would soon have been "hub-deep" and hopelessly stuck. So, too, with the carriages of the nabobs. The poorer people, when they travelled at all, went on foot or on horseback, as our ancestors did. The nabobs had their *volantes*, still occasionally, but with increasing rarity, seen in some parts of the island. Forty years ago, such vehicles, only a little changed from the original type, were common enough in Havana itself. About that time, or a few years earlier, the four-wheeler began to supplant them for city use.

There is a technical difference between the original type of *volante* and its successor which, though still called a *volante* was properly called a *quitrin*. The only real difference was that the top of the *quitrin* was collapsible, and could be lowered when desirable, while the top of the *volante* was not. I have ridden in these affairs, I cannot say comfortably, over roads that would have been quite impossible for any other wheeled vehicle. At the back, and somewhat behind the body were two wheels, six feet in diameter. From, the axle, two shafts projected for a distance, if memory serves me, of some twelve or fifteen feet. A little forward of the axle, the body, not unlike the old-fashioned American chaise, was suspended on stout leather straps serving as springs. Away off in front, at the end of the shafts, was a horse on which the driver rode in a heavy and clumsy saddle. For long-distance travel, or for particularly rough roads, a second horse was added, alongside the shaft horse, and sometimes a third animal. The motion was pleasant enough over the occasional smooth places, but the usual motion was much like that of a cork in a whirlpool, or of a small boat in a choppy sea. Little attention was paid to rocks or ruts; it was almost impossible to capsize the thing. One wheel might be two feet or more higher than the other, whereupon the rider on the upper side would be piled on top of the rider or riders on the lower side, but there was always a fair distribution of this favor. The rocks and ruts were not always on the same side of the road. The safety from overturn was in the long shafts which allowed free play. In the older days, say sixty or seventy years ago, the *volante* or the *quitrin* was an outward and visible sign of a well-lined pocket-book. It indicated the possessor as a man of wealth, probably a rich planter who needed such a vehicle to carry him and his family from their mansion in the city to their perhaps quite as costly home on the plantation. The *calisero*, or driver, was dressed in a costume truly gorgeous, the horses were of the best, and the vehicle itself may have cost two thousand dollars or more. The operation of such a contrivance, extending, from the rear of the wheels to the horse's nose, for twenty feet or more, in the narrow streets of the old city, was a scientific problem, particularly in turning corners.

Cuba was early in the field with a railway. In 1830, the United States had only thirty-two miles of line, the beginning of its present enormous system. Cuba's first railway was opened to traffic in November, 1837. It was a forty-five mile line connecting Havana with the town of Guines, southeast of the city. While official permission was, of course, necessary before the work could be undertaken, it was in fact a Cuban enterprise, due to the activity of the *Junta de Fomento*, or Society for Improvement. It was built with capital obtained in London, the construction being in charge of Mr. Alfred Cruger, an American engineer. Ten years later there were nearly three hundred miles of line. At the beginning of the American occupation, in 1899, there were about nine-hundred and fifty miles. There are now more than 2,000 miles of public service line in operation, and in addition there are many hundreds of miles of private lines on the sugar estates. Several cities have trolley lines. For some years after the American occupation, as before that experience, there was only a water-and-rail connection, or an all-water route, between the eastern and western sections of the island. The usual route from Havana to Santiago was by rail to Batabano or to Cienfuegos, and thence by steamer. The alternative was an all-water route, consuming several days, by steamer along the north coast, with halts at different ports, and around the eastern end of the island to the destination. It is now an all-rail run of twenty-four hours. The project for a "spinal railway" from one end of the island to the other had been under consideration for many years. The configuration lent itself excellently to such a system, and not at all well to any other. A railway map of such a system shows a line, generally, through the middle of the island along its length, with numerous branch lines running north and south to the various cities and ports on the coast. The plan, broadly, is being carried out. A combination of existing lines afforded a route to the city of Santa Clara. From these eastward, the Cuba Company, commonly known as the Van Home road, completed a through line in 1902. In its beginning, it was a highly ambitious scheme, involving the building of many towns along the way, the erection of many sugar mills, and the creation of a commercial city, at Nipe Bay, that would leave Havana in the back-number class. All that called for a sum of money not then and not now available. But the "spinal railroad" was built, and from it a number of radiating lines have been built, to Sancti Spiritus, Manzanillo, Nipe Bay, and to Guantanamo. About the only places on the island, really worth seeing, with the exception of Trinidad and Baracoa, can now be reached by a fairly comfortable railway journey.

In most of the larger cities of the island, a half dozen or so of them, the traveller is made fairly comfortable and is almost invariably well fed. But any question of physical comfort in hotels, more particularly in country hotels, raises a question of standards. As Touchstone remarked, when in the forest of Arden, "Travellers must be content." Those who are not ready to make themselves so, no matter what the surroundings, should stay at home, which, Touchstone also remarked, "is a better place." If the standard is the ostentatious structure of the larger cities of this country, with its elaborate menu and its systematized service, there will doubtless be cause for complaint. So will there be if the standard is the quiet, cleanly inn of many towns in this country and in parts of Europe. The larger towns and villages of the island have a *posada* in which food and lodging may be obtained; the smaller places may or may not have "a place to stay." Cuba is not a land in which commercial travellers swarm everywhere, demanding comfort and willing to pay a reasonable price for it. However, few travellers and fewer tourists have any inclination to depart from known and beaten paths, or any reason for doing so. Nor does a fairly thorough inspection of the island necessitate any halting in out-of-the-way places where there is not even an imitation of an inn. All that one needs to see, and all that most care to see, can be seen in little tours, for a day, from the larger cities. Yet if one wants to wander a little in the by-paths, it is easy enough to do so.

What one sees or does in Cuba will depend mainly upon the purpose of the visit, and upon the violence of the individual mania for seeing as many places as possible. If the object is merely an excursion or an escape from the rigors of a northern winter, there is no occasion for wandering out of sight of the capital city. There is more to see and more to do in Havana than there is in all the rest of the island. Nor is there much to be seen elsewhere that cannot be seen in the immediate vicinity of that city. This, of course, does not cover the matter of scenery. There are no mountains, no forest jungles in that neighborhood, but forests in Cuba are not particularly interesting, and even the mountains of Oriente are no more beautiful or majestic than are our own summits, our own White Hills of New Hampshire, the Adirondacks, the Blue Ridge, the Alleghenies, the Rockies, and the Sierras. The charm of Cuba, and it is extremely charming, is not its special "points of interest." It is rather a general impression, a combination of soft and genial climate with varying lights and shades and colors. Even after much experience there, I am not yet quite ready either to admit or to deny that the island, taken as a whole, is either beautiful or picturesque, and yet there is much of both. Attention is rarely challenged by the sublime or the majestic, but is often arrested by some play of light and shade. Cuban villages, with few exceptions, are unattractive, although there is not infrequently some particular building, usually a church, that calls for a second look or a careful examination. Most of these little communities consist of a row of low and ungraceful structures bordering the highway. They are usually extended by building on at the ends. If the town street gets undesirably long, a second street or a third will be made, on one or both sides of the main street, and thus the town acquires breadth as well as length. The houses are built immediately upon the roadside, and sidewalks are quite unusual. Nor, until the place becomes a large town or a small city, is there, in most cases, any attempt at decoration by means of shade trees. A tree may be left if there happened to be one when the village was born, but rarely do the inhabitants turn their streets into tree-shaded avenues. There would be an excellent opportunity for the activities of Village Improvement Societies in Cuba, if it were not for the fact that such tree-planting would involve pushing all the houses ten or fifteen feet back from the roadside.

I have never studied the system of town building in the island, yet it is presumable that there was some such system. In the larger places, there is usually a central park around which are arranged the church, the public buildings, and the stores. Whether these were so constructed from an original plan, or whether they are an evolution, along a general plan, from the long, single street, I do not know. I am inclined to believe that the former was the case, and that it followed the location of a church. The custom is, of course, of Spanish origin, and is common throughout the greater part of Latin America. It finds a fair parallel in our own country custom, by no means infrequent, of an open "green" or common in front of the village church and the town hall. Tree-setting along the Cuban highways, more particularly in the neighborhood of the cities, is not at all unusual, and some of these shaded roads are exceedingly charming. Some are entirely over-arched by laurel trees and the gorgeous *flamboyan*, making long tunnels of shade "through whose broken roof the sky looks in." Evidently the Spanish authorities were too much interested in making money and enjoying themselves in the cities to care very much for what happened to the Cubans in the villages, as long as they paid the money that filled the official pocket and paid for the official entertainment, and the Cubans were too busy getting that money to have much time for village improvement. The Spaniards, following their home custom, might decorate a military highway to some extent, but the rough trail over which the peasant carried his little crop did not concern them. That was quite the business of the peasant who had neither the time nor money to do anything about it.

The question of good roads in Cuba is very much what it is in this country. Cuba needs more good roads than its people can afford to build; so does the United States. At the time of the American occupation, in 1899, there were only 160 miles of improved highway in the entire island. Of this, 85 miles were in Havana Province, and 75 miles in Pinar del Rio. The remainder of the island had none. Some work was done during the First Intervention and more was done under the Palma government. At the time of the Second Intervention, there were about 380 miles. That is, the United States and the Cuban Republic built, in six years, nearly 40 per cent, more highway than the Spanish authorities built in four hundred years. During the Palma regime, plans were drawn for an extensive road system, to be carried out as rapidly as the financial resources permitted. Not unlike similar proceedings in this country, in river and harbor work and public buildings, politics came into the matter and, like our own under similar circumstances, each Congressman insisted that some of such work as could immediately be undertaken, some of the money that could be immediately spent, should benefit his particular district. The result was that what was done by the Cubans was somewhat scattered, short stretches built here and there, new bridges built when there might or might not be a usable road to them. The Cuban plan involved, for its completion, a period of years and a large appropriation. It called for comparatively small yearly appropriations for many roads, for more than four hundred different projects. Then came the Second Intervention, in 1906, with what has seemed to many of us an utterly unwise and unwarranted expenditure for the completion of certain selected projects included in the Cuban plan. It may be granted that the roads were needed, some of them very much needed, but there are thousands of miles of unconstructed but much needed roads in the United States. Yet, in this country, Federal, State, county, and town treasuries are not drained to their last dollar, and their credit strained, to build those roads. From the drain on its financial resources, the island will recover, but the misfortune appears in the setting of a standard for Federal expenditure, in its total for all purposes amounting to about $40,000,000 a year, far beyond the reasonable or proper bearing power of the island. But the work was done, the money spent, and the Cubans were committed to more work and to further expenditure. I find no data showing with exactness the mileage completed by the Magoon government, which came to an end in January, 1909, but a Cuban official report made at the end of 1910 shows that the combined activities of the respective administrations, Spanish, American, and Cuban, had given the island, at that time, practically a thousand miles of improved highway, distributed throughout the island.

To see the real Cuba, one must get into the country. Havana is the principal city, and for many it is the most interesting place on the island, but it is no more Cuba than Paris is France or than New York is the United States. The real Cuba is rural; the real Cuban is a countryman, a man of the soil. If he is rich, he desires to measure his possessions in *caballerias* of 33-1/3 acres; if poor, in *hectareas* of 2-1/2 acres. I do not recall any Cuban cartoon representing the Cuban people that was not a picture of the peasant, the *guajiro*. Cuba, as a political organism, is shown as a quite charming *senorita*, but *el pueblo Cubano*, the Cuban people, are shown as the man of the fields. With the present equipment of railroads, trolley lines, automobile busses, and highways, little excursions are easily made in a day. The railways, trolleys, and automobile busses are unsatisfactory means of locomotion for sight-seeing. The passenger is rushed past the very sights that would be of the greatest interest. To most of us, a private hired automobile is open to the very serious objection of its expensiveness, an item that may sometimes be reduced by division. It has been my good fortune in more recent years to be whirled around in cars belonging to friends but my favorite trip in earlier days is, I presume, still open to those who may care to make it. I have recommended it to many, and have taken a number with me over the route.

It is an easy one-day excursion of about sixty miles, by rail to Guanajay, by carriage to Marianao, and return to Havana by rail. Morning trains run to Guanajay, through a region generally attractive and certainly interesting to the novice, by way of Rincon and San Antonio de los Banos, a somewhat roundabout route, but giving a very good idea of the country, its plantations, villages, and peasant homes. At Guanajay, an early lunch, or a late breakfast, may be obtained at the hotel, before or after an inspection of the town itself, a typical place with its little central park, its old church, and typical residences. Inquiry regarding the transportation to Marianao by carriage should not be too direct. It should be treated as a mere possibility depending upon a reasonable charge. I have sometimes spent a very pleasant hour in intermittent bargaining with the competitors for the job, although knowing very well what I would pay and what they would finally accept. Amiably conducted, as such discussions should be in Cuba, the chaffering becomes a matter of mutual entertainment. A bargain concluded, a start may be made about noon for a drive over a good road, through a series of typical villages, to Marianao, in time for a late afternoon train to Havana, reaching there in ample time for dinner. Along the road from Guanajay to Marianao, Maceo swept with ruthless hand in 1896, destroying Spanish property. Here the Spaniards, no less ruthless, destroyed the property of Cubans. It is now a region of peaceful industry, and little or nothing remains to indicate its condition when I first saw it. The little villages along the way were in ruins, the fields were uncultivated, and there were no cattle. At intervals there stood the walls of what had been beautiful country estates. Only one of many was left standing. At intervals, also, stood the Spanish blockhouses. All along that route, in 1906, were the insurrectos of the unfortunate experience of that year. In the village of Caimito, a short distance from Guanajay, along that road, I visited Pino Guerra at his then headquarters when he and his forces so menaced Havana that Secretary Taft, in his capacity of Peace Commissioner, ordered their withdrawal to a greater distance. The trip by rail and road, exhibits most of Cuba's special characteristics. There are fields of sugar cane and fields of tobacco, country villages and peasant homes, fruits and vegetables, ceiba trees, royal palms, cocoanut palms, and mango trees. There is no other trip, as easily made, where so much can be seen. But there are other excursions in the vicinity, for many reasons best made by carriage or by private hired automobile. Within fifteen miles or so of the city, are places like Calvario, Bejucal, and Managua, all reached by good highways through interesting and typical country, and all well illustrating the real life of the real Cubans. It was in the vicinity of those places that Maximo Gomez operated in 1895 and 1896, terrorizing Havana by menacing it from the south and the east while Maceo threatened it from the west. Another short and pleasant trip can be made around the head of the harbor to Guanabacoa, and thence to Cojimar. Another interesting and easily reached point is Guines, a good example of places of its size and class.

Of Cuba's larger cities, there are a score that would demand attention in a guide-book. Just as there is a certain similarity in most American cities, in that they are collections of business and residence buildings of generally similar architecture, so is there a certain sameness in most of Cuba's cities. To see two or three of them is to get a general idea of all, although each has its particular features, some particular building, or some special charm of surroundings. The most difficult of access are Baracoa, the oldest city of the island, and Trinidad, founded only a few years later. Glancing at some of these places, in their order from west to east, the first is Pinar del Rio, a comparatively modern city, dating really from the second half of the 18th Century. It owes its past and its present importance to its location as a centre of the tobacco region of the *Vuelta Abajo*. From comfortable headquarters here, excursions can be made, by rail or road, through what is perhaps the most attractive, and not the least interesting section of the island. To the north are the Organ Mountains and the picturesque town of Vinales, one of the most charming spots, in point of scenery, in Cuba. To the west, by rail, is Guane, the oldest settlement in western Cuba, and all around are beautiful hills and cultivated valleys. Eastward from Havana, the first city of importance is Matanzas. Here is much to interest and much to charm, the city itself, its harbor, its two rivers, the famous valley of the Yumuri, and the caves of Bellamar. The city, founded in 1693, lies along the shore of the bay and rises to the higher ground of the hills behind it. It lies about sixty miles from Havana, and is easily reached by rail or by automobile. The next city in order, also on the north coast, is Cardenas, a modern place, settled in 1828, and owing its importance to its convenience as a shipping port for the numerous sugar estates in its vicinity, an importance now somewhat modified by the facilities for rail shipment to other harbors. Seventy-five miles or so further eastward is Sagua la Grande, another point of former convenience as a shipping point for sugar. The city itself is located on a river, or estuary, some ten or twelve miles from its mouth. Forty miles or so further on are Remedies and Caibarien, a few miles apart, the latter on the coast and the former a few miles inland. Caibarien, like Cardenas and Sagua, is chiefly notable as a sugar port, while Remedios is the centre of one of the great tobacco districts, producing a leaf of good quality but generally inferior to the *Partidos* of Havana Province, and quite inferior to the famous *Vuelta Abajo*. Southward of this region, and about midway the width of the island, somewhat more than two hundred miles eastward of Havana, is the city of Santa Clara, better known in the island as Villa Clara. The city dates its existence from 1689. It lies surrounded by rolling hills and expansive valleys, but in the absence of extensive plantations in its immediate environs, one is led to wonder just why so pleasant a place should be there, and why it should have reached its present proportions. For the tourist who wants to "see it all," it is an excellent and most comfortable central headquarters.

From Villa Clara it is only a short run to Cienfuegos, the "city of a hundred fires," a modern place, only about a hundred years old. There is every probability that Columbus entered the harbor in 1494, and perhaps no less probability that Ocampo entered in 1508, on his voyage around the island. The harbor extends inland for several miles, with an irregular shore line, behind which rises a border line of hills. The city itself is some four or five miles from the entrance to the harbor. It came into existence, and still exists, chiefly by reason of the sugar business. It is an important outlet for that industry, and many estates are in its near vicinity. The old city of Trinidad is reached, by boat, from Cienfuegos, or rather its port city, Casilda, is so reached. Presumably, it was the port city that

Velasquez founded in 1514, a location a few miles inland being chosen later, as being less exposed to attacks by the pirates and freebooters who infested the Caribbean Sea for many years. It is said that Cortes landed here and recruited his forces on his way to Mexico, in 1518. The city itself stands on the lower slopes of the hills that form its highly effective background. Its streets are narrow and tortuous. Like most of the cities of the island, and most of the cities of the world, it has its humble homes of the poor, and its mansions of the rich. Immediately behind it stands a hill with an elevation of about nine hundred feet above sea-level. Its name indicates the reason for its application, *La Vigia*, the "lookout," or the "watch-tower." From its summit, we may assume that the people of earlier times scanned the horizon for any sign of approaching pirates by whom they might be attacked. It serves a more satisfactory purpose nowadays in that it affords one of the loveliest panoramic views to be found anywhere in Cuba. Not far away, and accessible from the city, is the Pico de Potrerillo, about 3,000 feet elevation, the highest point in Central Cuba. Northeast of Trinidad, and reached by rail from Villa Clara, is Sancti Spiritus, Trinidad's rival in antiquity, both having been founded, by Velasquez, in the same year. Here also are narrow, crooked streets in a city of no mean attractions, although it lacks the picturesque charm of its rival in age. It is an inland city, about twenty-five miles from the coast, but even that did not protect it from attack by the pirates. It was several times the victim of their depredations.

VII

AROUND THE ISLAND: Continued

The next city, eastward, is Camaguey, in many ways doubtless the best worth a visit, next to Havana, of any city on the island. It is a place of interesting history and, for me personally, a place of somewhat mixed recollections. The history may wait until I have told my story. I think it must have been on my third visit to the island, early in 1902. On my arrival in Havana, I met my friend Charles M. Pepper, a fellow laborer in the newspaper field. He at once informed me that he and I were to start the next morning for a three or four weeks' journey around the island. It was news to me, and the fact that my baggage, excepting the suitcase that I carried, had failed to come on the boat that brought me, led me to demur. My objections were overruled on the ground that we could carry little baggage anyway, and all that was needed could be bought before starting, or along the way. The next morning saw us on the early train for Matanzas. We spent a week or ten days in that city, in Cardenas, Sagua, Santa Clara, and Cienfuegos, renewing former acquaintance and noting the changes effected by the restoration from the war period. That was before the completion of the Cuba Railway. To get to Camaguey, then known as Puerto Principe, we took the steamer at Cienfuegos and journeyed along the coast to Jucaro. There, because of shallow water, we were dropped into a shore boat some four or five miles from the coast, and there our troubles began. Fortunately, it was early morning. We got something to eat and some coffee, which is almost invariably good in Cuba, but when we meet nowadays we have a laugh over that breakfast at Jucaro. I don't know, and really don't care, what the place is now. After some hours of waiting, we secured passage in an antiquated little car attached to a freight train carrying supplies and structural material to Ciego de Avila, for use by the railway then being built in both directions, eastward and westward from that point. The line that there crosses the island from north to south was built in the time of the Ten Years' War (1868-1878) as a barrier against the revolutionists operating in eastern Cuba. It was restored for use in the revolution of 1895, but its blockhouses at every kilometre, and its barbed wire tangles, were entirely ineffective against Gomez and Maceo and other leaders, all of whom crossed it at their own sweet will, although not without an occasional vicious little contest. We reached Ciego de Avila soon after noon, and had to wait there over night for a further advance. The place is now a thriving little city, but it was then a somewhat sprawling village with a building that was called a hotel. But we got food and drink and beds, all that is really necessary for experienced campaigners. For the next two days, Old Man Trouble made himself our personal companion and did not lose sight of us for a single minute.

Through personal acquaintance with the railway officials, we obtained permission to travel over the line, on any and all trains, as far as it was then built, some forty miles or so toward Camaguey. Through them, also, we arranged for saddle horses to meet us at railhead for the remainder of the journey. There were no trains except construction trains carrying rails, ties, lumber, and other materials. We boarded the first one out in the morning. We had our choice of riding on any of those commodities that we might select. There was not even a caboose. We chose a car of lumber as the most promising. For four or five hours we crawled through that country, roasting and broiling on that pile of planks, but the ties and the rails were even hotter. The only way we could keep a place cool enough to sit on was by sitting on it. I once occupied a stateroom next to the steamer's funnel. I have seen, day after day, the pitch bubble between the planks of a steamer's deck in the Indian Ocean. I have been in other places that I thought plenty hot enough, but never have I been so thoroughly cooked as were my companion and I perched on the lumber pile. On top of that, or rather on top of us, there poured a constant rain of cinders from the locomotive puffing away a few cars ahead of us. The road-bed was rough, and at times we had to hang on for our very lives. We can laugh about it now, but, at the time, it was no joke. At last we reached the end of the line, somewhere in a hot Cuban forest, but there were no horses. We watched the operation of railway building, and took turns in anathematizing, in every language of which we had any knowledge, the abandoned ruffian who failed to appear with those horses. Before night, we were almost ready to wish that he had died on the way. At last he came. Our baggage was loaded on a pack-horse; we mounted and rode gallantly on our way. We had about thirty miles to cover by that or some other means of locomotion. Before we had gone a mile, we developed a clear understanding of the reasons for the sale of those horses by the Government of the United States, but why the United States Army ever bought them for cavalry mounts we could not even imagine. There was no road. Most of the way we followed the partly constructed road-bed for the new railway, making frequent detours, through field or jungle, to get around gaps or places of impossible roughness. Before we had covered two miles, we began to wish that the man who sent those horses, a Spaniard, by the way, might be doomed to ride them through all eternity under the saddles with which they were equipped. We were sorry enough for the poor brutes, but sorrier still for ourselves. For several days, I limped in misery from a long row of savage blisters raised on my leg by rawhide knots with which my saddle had been repaired. An hour after starting, we were overtaken by a heavy thunder-shower. At nightfall, after having covered about fifteen wretched miles, we reached a construction camp where an American nobleman, disguised as a section-boss, gave us food and lodging in the little palm-leaf shack that served as his temporary home. It was barely big enough for one, but he made it do for three.

Early in the morning, we resumed our journey, plodding along as best we could over a half-graded "right-of-way." A couple of hours brought us to a larger construction camp where we halted for such relief as we could secure. We then were some twelve or fourteen miles from our destination. We discussed the wisdom of making the rest of the way on foot, as preferable to that particular kind of saddle-work, leaving our baggage to come along with the horses when it might. But fortune smiled, or it may have been just a grimace. Word came that a team, two horses and a wagon, would go to the city that afternoon, and there would be room for us. We told our pilot, the man with the horses, just what we thought of him and all his miserable ancestors, gave him a couple of *pesos*, and rejoiced over our prospects of better fortune. But it proved to be only an escape from the fire into the frying-pan. I have driven over many miles of South African *veldt*, straight "across lots," in all comfort, but while the general topography of Camaguey puts it somewhat into the *veldt* class, its immediate surface did not in the least remind me of the South African plateau. The trip was little short of wonderful for its bumpiness. We got to Camaguey sore and bruised but, as far as we could discover, physically intact, and, having arrived, may now return to its history and description. May no "gentle reader" who scans these pages repeat our experience in getting there. It is supposed that here, or immediately here-about, was the place of "fifty houses and a thousand people" encountered by the messengers of Columbus, when he sent them inland to deliver official letters of introduction to the gorgeous ruler of the country in which he thought he was. Different writers tell different stories about the settlement of the place, but there is no doubt that it was among the earliest to be settled. Columbus gave to a harbor in that vicinity, in all probability the Bay of Nuevitas, the name Puerto del Principe, or Port of the Prince. He called the islands of the neighborhood the Gardens of the King. On that bay, about 1514, Diego Velasquez founded a city, probably the present Nuevitas, which he is said to have called Santa Maria. Somewhere from two to ten years later, an inland settlement was made. This developed into the city that was afterward given the name of Santa Maria del Puerto del Principe, now very properly changed to the old Indian name of Camaguey.

If the idea of an inland location was, as it is said to have been, protection against pirates and buccaneers, it was not altogether a success. The distinguished pirate, Mr. Henry Morgan, raided the place very effectively in 1668, securing much loot. In his book, published in 1871, Mr. Hazard says: "Puerto Principe (the present Camaguey) is, probably, the oldest, quaintest town on the island,— in fact, it may be said to be a finished town, as the world has gone on so fast that the place seems a million years old, and from its style of dress, a visitor might think he was put back almost to the days of Columbus." There have been changes since that time, but the old charm is still there, the narrow and crooked streets, forming almost a labyrinth, the old buildings, and much else that I earnestly hope may never be changed. There is now an up-to-date hotel, connected with the railway company, but if I were to go there again and the old hotel was habitable, I know I should go where I first stayed, and where we occupied a huge barrack-like room charged on our bill as "*habitaciones preferentes*," the state chamber. It had a dirty tiled floor, and was the home of many fleas, but there was something about it that I liked. I do not mean to say that all of Camaguey, "the city of the plain," is lovely, or picturesque or even interesting. No more is all of Paris, or Budapest, or Amsterdam, or Washington. They are only so in some of their component parts, but it is those parts that remain in the memory. The country around the city is a vast plain, for many years, and still, a grazing country, a land of horses and cattle. The charm is in the city itself. If I could see only one place outside of Havana, I would see Camaguey. A little less than fifty miles to the north is Nuevitas, reached by one of the first railways built in Cuba, now if ever little more than the port city for its larger neighbor. Columbus became somewhat ecstatic over the region. Perhaps it was then more charming, or the season more favorable, than when I saw it. I do not recall any feeling of special enthusiasm about its scenic charms. Perhaps I should have discovered them had I stayed longer. Perhaps I should have been more impressed had it not been for the impressions of Camaguey. I saw Nuevitas only briefly on my way eastward on that memorable excursion by construction train and saddle. The only route then available was by boat along the north shore, and it was there that we caught the steamer for Santiago.

That sail along the coast would have afforded greater pleasure had it lacked the noisy presence of an itinerant opera company whose members persisted, day and night, in exercising their lungs to the accompaniment of an alleged piano in the cabin. I have a far more pleasant recollection, or rather a memory because it stays with me, of music in those waters. The transport on which I went to Porto Rico, in the summer of 1898, carried, among other troops, a battery of light artillery. It had an unusually good bugler, and his sounding of "taps" on those soft, starlit nights remains with me as one of the sweetest sounds I have ever heard. The shrieks, squalls, and roars of those opera people were in a wholly different class. About seventy-five miles east of Nuevitas is Gibara, merely a shipping port for the inland city of Holguin. The former is only one of a number of such places found along the coast. Most of them are attractive in point of surrounding scenery, but little or not at all attractive in themselves, being mere groups of uninteresting structures of the conventional type. Holguin is perhaps two hundred years old, quite pleasantly situated, but affording no special points of interest for the tourist. The city is now easily reached by a branch of the Cuba Railway. It is worth the visit of those who "want to see it all." Beyond Gibara is Nipe Bay, not improbably the first Cuban harbor entered by Columbus. Nipe Bay and its near neighbor, Banes Bay, are the centres of what is now the greatest industrial activity of any part of the island. Here, recent American investment is measured in scores of millions of dollars. Here, in the immediate neighborhood, are some of the largest sugar plantations and mills on the island, the Boston and the Preston. A little to the west of Gibara are two others, Chaparra and Delicias. Hitherto, the western half of the island has been, the great producing district, but present indications point to a not distant time when the eastern district will rival and, it may be, outstrip the section of older development. The foundation is already laid for an extensive enterprise. Nature has afforded one of the finest land-locked harbors in the world at Nipe, and another, though smaller, a few miles away, at Banes. The region now has railroad connection with practically all parts of the island. Around those bays are sugar lands, tobacco lands, fruit lands, and a few miles inland are the vast iron ore beds that, as they are developed, will afford employment for an army of workmen. Nipe Bay is the natural commercial outlet for a vast area of richly productive soil. At present, the region affords nothing of special interest except its industrial activities, its miles and miles of sugar cane, its huge mills, and the villages built to house its thousands of workmen.

Seventy-five miles or so eastward of Nipe, lies one of the most charming and interesting spots on the island. This is old Baracoa, the oldest settlement on the island, now to be reached only by water or by the roughest of journeys over mountain trails. The town itself does not amount to much, but the bay is a gem, a little, circular basin, forest-shaded to its border, its waters clear as crystal. Behind it rise the forest-clad hills, step on step, culminating in *el Yunque*, "the anvil," with an elevation of about eighteen hundred feet. Baracoa is supposed to be the place about which Columbus wrote one of his most glowing and extravagant eulogies. Whether it is really worth the time and the discomfort of a special trip to see it, is perhaps somewhat doubtful. It is a place of scenery and sentiment, and little else. There is an old fort on a hilltop, not particularly picturesque, and an old church in which is a cross quite doubtfully reported as having been furnished by Columbus. Sometime, years hence, there will be easier communication, and the fertile hillsides and still more fertile valleys will supply various produces for consumption in the United States. About twenty-five miles east of Baracoa is the end of the island, Cape Maisi. Swinging around that, the coasting steamers turn due west along the shore to Santiago, passing the harbor of Guantanamo, with its United States naval station. That place is reached by rail from Santiago, a highly picturesque route through the Guantanamo valley. Besides the naval station, the place is a shipping port, affording nothing of special interest to the traveller who has seen other and more easily accessible cities of its type. It always seems to me that Santiago, or more properly Santiago de Cuba, would be more engaging if we could forget the more recent history of this city, known to most Cubans as Cuba (pronounced Cooba). No doubt, it is a much better place in which to live than it was twenty years ago, and much of its old charm remains. Its setting cannot be changed. It is itself a hillside town, surrounded by hills, with real mountains on its horizon. The old cathedral, a dominant structure, has been quite a little patched up in recent years, and shows the patches. The houses, big and little, are still painted in nearly all the shades of the spectrum. But there is a seeming change, doubtless psychological rather than physical. One sees, in imagination, Cervera's squadron "bottled up" in the beautiful harbor, while Sampson's ships lie outside waiting for it to come out. It is difficult to forget San Juan Hill and El Caney, a few miles behind the city, and remember only its older stories. A good deal of history has been made here in the last four hundred years. Its pages show such names as Velasquez, Grijalva, Hernan Cortes, and Narvaez, and centuries later, Cespedes, Marti, and Palma. Here was enacted the grim tragedy of the *Virginius*, and here was the conflict that terminated Spain's once vast dominion in the western world. My own impression is that most of its history has already been written, that it will have no important future. As a port of shipment, I think it must yield to the new port, Nipe Bay, on the north coast. It is merely a bit of commercial logic, the question of a sixty-mile rail-haul as compared with a voyage around the end of the island.

Santiago will not be wiped from the map, but I doubt its long continuance as the leading commercial centre of eastern Cuba. It is also a fairly safe prediction that the same laws of commercial logic will some day operate to drain northward the products of the fertile valley of the Cauto, and the region behind old Manzanillo and around the still older Bayamo.

Except the places earlier mentioned, Jucaro, Trinidad and Cienfuegos, there are no southern ports to the west until Batabano is reached, immediately south of, and only a few miles from, the city of Havana. It is a shallow harbor, of no commercial importance. It serves mainly as the centre of a sponge-fishing industry, and as a point of departure for the Isle of Pines, and for ports on the south coast. The Isle of Pines is of interest for a number of reasons, among which are its history, its mineral springs, its delightful climate, and an American colony that has made much trouble in Washington. Columbus landed there in 1494, and gave it the name *La Evangelista*. It lies about sixty miles off the coast, almost due south from Havana. Between the island and the mainland lies a labyrinth of islets and keys, many of them verdure-clad. Its area is officially given as 1,180 square miles. There seems no doubt that, at some earlier time, it formed a part of the main island, with which it compares in geologic structure and configuration. It is now, in effect, two islands connected by a marsh; the northern part being broken and hilly, and the southern part low, flat, and sandy, probably a comparatively recently reclaimed coralline plain. The island has been, at various times, the headquarters of bands of pirates, a military hospital, a penal institution, and a source of political trouble. It is now a Cuban island the larger part of which is owned by Americans. It is a part of the province of Havana, and will probably so remain as long as Cuba is Cuba. My personal investigations of the disputed question of the political ownership of the island began early in 1899. I then reached a conclusion from which I have not since seen any reason to depart. The island was then, had always been, and is now, as much a part of Cuba as Long Island and Key West have been and are parts of the United States.

Just who it was that first raised the question of ownership, none of us who investigated the matter at the time of its particular acuteness, was able to determine satisfactorily, although some of us had a well-defined suspicion. The man is now dead, and I shall not give his name. Article I, of the Treaty of Paris, of December 10, 1898, presumably disposes of the Cuban area; Article II refers to Porto Rico; and Article III refers to the Philippines. The issue regarding the Isle of Pines was raised under Article II, presumably referring only to Porto Rico. A slight but possibly important difference appears in the Spanish and the English versions. The English text reads that "Spain cedes ...the island of Porto Rico and other islands now under Spanish sovereignty" etc. The Spanish text, literally translated runs: "Spain cedes... the island of Porto Rico and the others that are now under its sovereignty." The obvious reference of the article is to Mona, Viequez, and Culebra, all small islands in Porto Rican waters. But the question was raised and was vigorously discussed. An official map was issued showing the island as American territory. Americans jumped in, bought up large tracts, and started a lively real estate boom. They advertised it widely as

American territory, and many put their little collections of dollars into it. The claim of Spanish cession was afterward denied in the very document that served to keep the issue alive for a number of years. Article VI of the Platt Amendment, which the Cubans accepted with marked reluctance, declared that the island was omitted from the boundaries of Cuba, and that the title and ownership should be left to future adjustment by treaty. But no alternative appears between cession and no cession. Had the island become definitely American territory by cession, its alienation, by such a step, would not have been possible. When we left Cuba, in 1902, the official instructions from Washington were that the Isle of Pines would remain under a *de facto* American government. President Palma, accepting the transfer, expressed his understanding that it would "continue *de facto* under the jurisdiction of the Republic of Cuba." In some way, the departing American authority failed to leave any agent or representative of the *de facto* government of the United States, and the Cubans included the island in their new administration, very properly. When the treaty proposed by the Platt Amendment came before the United States Senate, it hung fire, and finally found lodgment in one of the many pigeon-holes generously provided for the use of that august body. There it may probably be found today, a record and nothing more. Why? For the very simple reason that some of the resident claimants for American ownership sent up a consignment of cigars made on the island from tobacco grown on the island, and refused to pay duty on them. The ground of refusal was that they were a domestic product, sent from one port in the United States to another port in the same country, and therefore not dutiable. The case of Pearcy *vs* Stranahan, the former representing the shippers, and the latter being the Collector of the Port of New York, came before the Supreme Court of the United States, and that final authority decided and declared that the Isle of Pines was Cuban territory and a part of Cuba. The question is settled, and the Isle of Pines can become territory of the United States only by purchase, conquest, or some other form of territorial transfer.

While the American settlers in the Isle of Pines, and the several real-estate companies who seek purchasers for their holdings, own a large part of the territory, they still constitute a minority of the population. Many of the settlers, probably most of them, are industrious and persistent in their various productive activities. Their specialty is citrus fruits, but their products are not limited to that line. More than a few have tried their little experiment in pioneering, and have returned to their home land more or less disgusted with their experience. Those who have remained, and have worked faithfully and intelligently, have probably done a little better than they would have done at home. The great wealth for which all, doubtless, earnestly hoped, and in which many, doubtless, really believed, has not come. This settlement is only one of many speculative exploitations in Cuba. Some of these have been fairly honest, but many of them have been little better than rank swindles. Many have been entirely abandoned, the buyers losing the hard-earned dollars they had invested. Others, better located, have been developed, by patience, persistence, and thrift, into fairly prosperous colonies. I do not know how many victims have been caught by unscrupulous and ignorant promoters in the last fifteen years, principally in the United States and in Canada, but they are certainly many, so many that the speculative industry has declined in recent years. Many of the settlers who have remained have learned the game, have discovered that prosperity in Cuba is purchased by hard work just as it is elsewhere. In different parts of the island, east, west, and centre, there are now thrifty and contented colonists who have fought their battle, and have learned the rules that nature has formulated as the condition of success in such countries. Whether these people have really done any better than they would have done had they stayed at home and followed the rules there laid down, is perhaps another question. At all events, there are hundreds of very comfortable and happy American homes in Cuba, even in the Isle of Pines, where they persist in growling because it is Cuba and not the United States.

In a review of a country including forty-four thousand square miles of territory, condensed into two chapters, it is quite impossible to include all that is worth telling. Moreover, there is much in the island of which no adequate description can be given. There is much that must be seen if it if to be fairly understood and appreciated.

VIII

THE UNITED STATES AND CUBA

IN his message to Congress, on December 5, 1898, President McKinley declared that "the new Cuba yet to arise from the ashes of the past must needs be bound to us by ties of singular intimacy and strength if its enduring welfare is to be assured."

Probably to many of the people of the United States, the story of our relations with Cuba had its beginning with the Spanish-American war. That is quite like a notion that the history of an apple begins with its separation from the tree on which it grew. The general history of the island is reviewed in other chapters in this volume. The story of our active relations with Cuba and its affairs runs back for more than a hundred years, at least to the days of President Thomas Jefferson who, in 1808, wrote thus to Albert Gallatin: "I shall sincerely lament Cuba's falling into any other hands but those of its present owners." Several other references to the island appear at about that time. Two great movements were then going on. Europe was in the throes of the Napoleonic disturbance, and for more than twenty-five years both France and England schemed, sometimes openly and sometimes secretly, for the possession of Cuba. The other movement was the revolution in Spain's colonies in the Western Hemisphere, a movement that cost Spain all of its possessions in that area, with the exception of Cuba and Porto Rico. The influence of the revolutionary activities naturally extended to Cuba, but it was not until after 1820 that matters became dangerously critical. From that time until the present, the question of Cuba's political fate, and the question of our relations with the island, form an interesting and highly important chapter in the history of the United States as well as in the history of Cuba.

In his book on the war with Spain, Henry Cabot Lodge makes a statement that may seem curious to some and amazing to others. It is, however, the opinion of a competent and thoroughly trained student of history. He writes thus:

"The expulsion of Spain from the Antilles is merely the last and final step of the inexorable movement in which the United States has been engaged for nearly a century. By influence and by example, or more directly, by arms and by the pressure of ever-advancing settlements, the United States drove Spain from all her continental possessions in the Western Hemisphere, until nothing was left to the successors of Charles and Philip but Cuba and Porto Rico. How did it happen that this great movement stopped when it came to the ocean's edge? The movement against Spain was at once national and organic, while the pause on the sea-coast was artificial and in contravention of the laws of political evolution in the Americas. The conditions in Cuba and Porto Rico did not differ from those which had gone down in ruin wherever the flag of Spain waved on the mainland. The Cubans desired freedom, and Bolivar would fain have gone to their aid. Mexico and Colombia, in 1825, planned to invade the island, and at that time invasion was sure to be successful. What power stayed the oncoming tide which had swept over a continent? Not Cuban loyalty, for the expression 'Faithful Cuba' was a lie from the beginning. The power which prevented the liberation of Cuba was the United States, and more than seventy years later this republic has had to fight a war because at the appointed time she set herself against her own teachings, and brought to a halt the movement she had herself started to free the New World from the oppression of the Old. The United States held back Mexico and Colombia and Bolivar, used her influence at home and abroad to that end, and, in the opinion of contemporary mankind, succeeded, according to her desires, in keeping Cuba under the dominion of Spain."

For a number of years, Cuba's destiny was a subject of the gravest concern in Washington. Four solutions presented themselves; first, the acquisition of Cuba by the United States; second, its retention by Spain; third, its transfer to some power other than Spain; fourth, its political independence. That the issue was decided by the United States is shown by all the history of the time. While other factors had their influence in the determination, it is entirely clear that the issue turned on the question of slavery. In his book on *Cuba and International Relations*, Mr. Callahan summarizes his review of the official proceedings by saying that "the South did not want to see Cuba independent *without* slavery, while the North did not want to annex it *with* slavery." In his work on the *Rise and Fall of the Slave Power in America*, Mr. Henry Wilson declares that "thus clearly and unequivocally did this Republic step forth the champion of slavery, and boldly insist that these islands should remain under the hateful despotism of Spain, rather than gain their independence by means that should inure to the detriment of its cherished system. Indeed, it (the United States) would fight to fasten more securely the double bondage on Cuba and the slave."

From this point of view, unquestionably correct, it is altogether evident that the United States assumed responsibility for Cuba's welfare, not by the intervention of 1898, but by its acts more than seventy years earlier. The diplomatic records of those years are filled with communications regarding the island, and it was again and again the subject of legislation or proposed legislation. President after President dealt with it in messages to Congress. The acquisition of the island, by purchase or otherwise, was again and again discussed. Popular interest was again and again excited; the Spanish colonial policy was denounced; and the burdens and sufferings of the Cubans were depicted in many harrowing tales. For the policy that led to the imposition of a restraining hand on proposals to free Cuba, in those early days, the people of the United States today must blush. The independence movement in the States of Spanish-America may be said to have had its definite beginning in 1806, when Francisco Miranda, a Venezuelan, sailed from New York with three ships manned by American filibusters, although the first land battle was fought in Bolivia, in 1809, and the last was fought in the same country, in 1825. But the great wave swept from the northern border of Mexico to the southernmost point of Spanish possession. When these States declared their independence, they wrote into their Constitutions that all men should be free, that human slavery should be abolished forever from their soil. The attitude of the United States in the matter of Cuba was determined by the objection to the existence of an anti-slavery State so near our border. The experience of Haiti and Santo Domingo was, of course, clearly in mind, but the objection went deeper than that. Those who are interested may read with profit the debates in the Congress of the United States, in 1826, on the subject of the despatch of delegates to the so-called Panama Congress-of that year. On the whole, it is not pleasant reading from any present point of view.

Our cherished Monroe Doctrine was one of the fruits of this period, and in the enunciation of that policy the affairs of Cuba were a prominent if not the dominant force. The language of this doctrine is said to have been written by Secretary Adams, but it is embodied in the message of President Monroe, in December, 1823, and so bears his name. In April, of that year, Secretary Adams sent a long communication to Mr. Nelson, then the American Minister to Spain. For their bearing on the Cuban question, and for the presentation of a view that runs through many years of American policy, extracts from that letter may be included here.

DEPARTMENT OF STATE,
WASHINGTON, April 28, 1823.

"In the war between France and Spain, now commencing, other interests, peculiarly ours, will, in all probability, be deeply involved. Whatever may be the issue of this war, as between these two European powers, it may be taken for granted that the dominion of Spain upon the American continent, north and south, is irrecoverably gone. But the islands of Cuba and Porto Rico still remain nominally, and so far really, dependent upon her, that she possesses the power of transferring her own dominion over them, together with the possession of them, to others. These islands, from their local position are natural appendages to the North American continent, and one of them, Cuba, almost in sight of our shores, from a multitude of considerations, has become an object of transcendant importance to the commercial and political interests of our Union. Its commanding position, with reference to the Gulf of Mexico and the West India seas; the character of its population; its situation midway between our southern coast and the island of St. Domingo; its safe and capacious harbor of the Havana, fronting a long line of our shores destitute of the same advantage; the nature of its productions and of its wants, furnishing the supplies and needing the returns of a commerce immensely profitable and mutually beneficial,—give it an importance in the sum of our national interests with which that of no other foreign territory can be compared, and little inferior to that which binds the different members of this Union together. Such, indeed, are the interests of that island and of this country, the geographical, commercial, moral, and political relations, that, in looking forward to the probable course of events, for the short period of half a century, it is scarcely possible to resist the conviction that the annexation of Cuba to our federal republic will be indispensable to the continuance and integrity of the Union itself."

The communication proceeds to relate the knowledge of the Department that both Great Britain and France were desirous of securing possession and control of the island, and to disclaim, on the part of the United States, all disposition to obtain possession of either Cuba or Porto Rico. The complications of the situation became increasingly serious, more particularly with regard to Cuba, and on December 2, of that year (1823), President Monroe issued his message carrying the "doctrine," which may be given thus:

"In the wars of the European powers in matters relating to themselves we have never taken any part, nor does it comport with our policy to do so. It is only when our rights are invaded or seriously menaced that we resent injuries or make preparations for our defense. With the movements in this hemisphere we are of necessity more immediately connected. We owe it, therefore, to candor and to the amicable relations existing between the United States and those powers (of Europe) to declare that we should consider any attempt on their part to extend their system to any portion of this hemisphere as dangerous to our peace and safety. With the existing colonies or dependencies of any European power we have not interfered and shall not interfere. But with the Governments that have declared their independence and maintained it, and whose independence we have recognized, we could not view any interposition for the purpose of oppressing them, or controlling in any other manner their destiny, by any European power in any other light than as the manifestation of an unfriendly disposition toward the United States."

From this time onward, Cuba appears as an almost continuous object of special interest to both the people and the officials of the United States. Notwithstanding this disclaimer of President Monroe's message, the idea of the acquisition of the island, by the United States, soon arose. It persisted through all the years down to the time of the Teller amendment, in 1898, and there are many who even now regard annexation as inevitable at some future time, more or less distant. The plan appears as a suggestion in a communication, under date of November 30, 1825, from Alexander H. Everett, then Minister to Madrid, to President Adams. It crops up repeatedly in various quarters in later years. It would be a difficult and tedious undertaking to chase through all the diplomatic records of seventy years the references to Cuba and its affairs.

From that period until the present time, the affairs of the island have been a matter of constant interest and frequent anxiety in Washington. Fear of British acquisition of the island appears to have subsided about 1860, but there were in the island two groups, both relatively small, one of them working for independence, and the other for annexation to the United States. The great majority, however, desired some fair measure of self-government, and relief from economic and financial burdens, under the Spanish flag. The purchase of the island by the United States was proposed by President Polk, in 1848; by President Pierce, in 1854; and by President Buchanan, in his time. Crises appeared from time to time. Among them was the incident of the *Black Warrior*, in 1854. Mr. Rhodes thus describes the affair, in his *History of the United States*:

"*The Black Warrior* was an American merchant steamer, plying between Mobile and New York, stopping at Havana for passengers and mail. She had made thirty-six such voyages, almost always having a cargo for the American port, and never being permitted to bring freight into Havana. The custom of her agent was to clear her 'in ballast' the day before her arrival. The practice, while contrary to the regulations of Cuban ports, had always been winked at by the authorities. It was well understood that the *Black Warrior* generally had a cargo aboard, but a detailed manifest of her load had never been required. She had always been permitted to sail unmolested until, when bound from Mobile to New York, she was stopped on the 28th of February, 1854, by order of the royal exchequer, for having violated the regulations of the port. The agent, finding that the cause of this proceeding was the failure to manifest the cargo 'in transit,' offered to amend the manifest, which under the rules he had a right to do; but this the collector, on a flimsy pretext, refused to permit. The agent was at the same time informed that the cargo was confiscated and the captain fined, in pursuance of the custom-house regulations. The cargo was cotton, valued at one hundred thousand dollars; and the captain was fined six thousand dollars. The United States consul applied to the captain-general for redress, but no satisfaction was obtained. A gang of men with lighters were sent to the ship under the charge of the *commandante*, who ordered the captain of the *Black Warrior* to discharge her cargo. This he refused to do. The *commandante* then had the hatches opened, and his men began to take out the bales of cotton. The captain hauled down his flag and abandoned the vessel to the Spanish authorities."

The news of the incident created great excitement in Washington. President Pierce sent a message to Congress, stating that demand had been made on Spain for indemnity, and suggesting provisional legislation that would enable him, if negotiations failed, "to insure the observance of our just rights, to obtain redress for injuries received, and to vindicate the honor of our flag."

Mr. Soule, then the American Minister to Madrid, was the official through whom the negotiations were conducted. He was a man of somewhat impetuous temperament, and an ardent advocate of Cuba's annexation. He quite overstepped both the bounds of propriety and of his authority in his submission, under instructions, of a demand for three hundred thousand dollars indemnity. This, and Spanish diplomatic methods, led to delay, and the excitement died out. In the meantime, Spain released the vessel and its cargo, disavowed and disapproved the conduct of the local officials, paid the indemnity claimed by the owners of the vessel, and the ship resumed its regular trips, being treated with every courtesy when visiting Havana. But the incident gave rise to active discussion, and for a time threatened serious results. It followed on the heels of another experience, the Lopez expeditions, to which reference is made in another chapter, and came at a time when Cuba and Cuban affairs were topics of a lively public interest. The subject of acquisition was under general public discussion and occupied a large share of public attention. Some wanted war with Spain, and others proposed the purchase of the island from Spain. But the immediate cause of complaint having been removed by the release of the ship, Soule was instructed to take no further steps in the matter, and the excitement gradually passed away.

Immediately following this experience, and growing out of it, came the incident of the "Ostend Manifesto." At that time, James Buchanan was Minister to England. John Y. Mason was Minister to France, and Pierre Soule was Minister to Spain. Secretary of State Marcy suggested a conference between these three officials. They met at Ostend, but afterward transferred their deliberations to Aix la Chapelle. The meeting attracted general attention in Europe. The result of what they reported as "a full and unreserved interchange of views and sentiments," was a recommendation that an earnest effort be made immediately to purchase Cuba. They were of opinion that the sum of one hundred and twenty million dollars be offered. The report proceeded thus: "After we shall have offered Spain a price for Cuba far beyond its present value, and this shall have been refused, it will then be time to consider the question, does Cuba in the possession of Spain seriously endanger our internal peace and the existence of our cherished Union? Should this question be answered in the affirmative, then, by every law, human and divine, we shall be justified in wresting it from Spain if we possess the power; and this upon the very same principle that would justify an individual in tearing down the burning house of his neighbor if there were no other means of preventing the flame from destroying his own home." It is evident that Soule dominated the meeting, and only less evident that he, in some way, cajoled his associates into signing the report. No action was taken on the matter by the Administration, and the incident has passed into history somewhat, perhaps, as one of the curiosities of diplomacy. At all events, all historians note it, and some give it considerable attention.

The next serious complication arose out of the Ten Years' War, in Cuba, in 1868, to which reference is made in a chapter on Cuba's revolutions. Spain's leaders seemed quite incapable of grasping the Cuban situation, of seeing it in its proper light. It is more than probable that, even then, the Cubans would have remained loyal if the Spanish authorities had paid attention to their just and reasonable demands. As stated by Mr. Pepper, in his *Tomorrow in Cuba*, "The machete and the torch then gained what peaceful agitation had not been able to achieve." The demands of the Cubans are thus stated by Señor Cabrera, in his *Cuba and the Cubans*: "A constitutional system in place of the autocracy of the Captain-General, freedom of the press, the right of petition, cessation of the exclusion of Cubans from public office, unrestricted industrial liberty, abolition of restrictions on the transfer of landed property, the right of assembly and of association, representation in the Cortes, and local self-government," all reasonable and just demands from every point of view of modern civilization. Spain refused all, and on October 10, 1868, an actual revolution began, the first in the history of the island to be properly classed as a revolution. The United

States soon became concerned and involved. In his message to Congress on December 6, 1869, President Grant said: "For more than a year, a valuable province of Spain, and a near neighbor of ours, in whom all our people cannot but feel a deep interest, has been struggling for independence and freedom. The people and the Government of the United States entertain the same warm feelings and sympathies for the people of Cuba in their pending struggle that they have manifested throughout the previous struggles between Spain and her former colonies (Mexico, Central America and South America) in behalf of the latter. But the contest has at no time assumed the conditions which amount to a war in the sense of international law, or which would show the existence of a *de facto* political organization of the insurgents sufficient to justify a recognition of belligerency." On June 13, 1870, President Grant sent a special message to Congress, in which he reviewed the Cuban situation. Another reference appears in his message of December 5, 1870. In his message of December 4, 1871, he stated that "it is to be regretted that the disturbed condition of the island of Cuba continues to be a source of annoyance and anxiety. The existence of a protracted struggle in such close proximity to our own territory, without apparent prospect of an early termination, cannot be other than an object of concern to a people who, while abstaining from interference in the affairs of other powers, naturally desire to see every other country in the undisturbed enjoyment of peace, liberty, and the blessings of free institutions." In the message of December 2, 1872, he said: "It is with regret that I have again to announce a continuance of the disturbed condition in the island of Cuba. The contest has now lasted for more than four years. Were its scene at a distance from our neighborhood, we might be indifferent to its result, although humanity could not be unmoved by many of its incidents wherever they might occur. It is, however, at out door." Reference was made to it in all following annual messages, until President Hayes, in 1878, announced its termination, ten years after its beginning. The contest had become practically a deadlock, and a compromise was arranged by General Maximo Gomez, for the Cubans, and General Martinez Campos, for Spain.

The entanglements that grew out of the experiences of this period are too long and too complicated for detailed review here. This country had no desire for war with Spain, but approval of the Spanish policy in Cuba was impossible. The sympathies of the American people were with the Cubans, as they had been for fifty years, and as they continued to be until the end of Spanish occupation in the West Indies. Rumors of all kinds were afloat, and again and again the situation seemed to have reached a crisis that could be ended only by war. A particularly aggravating incident appeared in what is known as the *Virginius* case. This was described as follows, in President Grant's message to Congress on December 1, 1873.

"The steamer *Virginius* was on the 26th day of September, 1870, duly registered at the port of New York as a part of the commercial marine of the United States. On the 4th of October, 1870, having received the certificate of her register in the usual legal form, she sailed from the port of New York, and has not since been within the territorial jurisdiction of the United States. On the 31st day of October last (1873), while sailing under the flag of the United States on the high seas, she was forcibly seized by the Spanish gunboat *Tornado*, and was carried into the port of Santiago de Cuba, where fifty-three of her passengers and crew were inhumanly, and, so far at least as related to those who were citizens of the United States, without due process of law, put to death."

Only for the timely arrival of the British man-of-war *Niobe*, and the prompt and decisive action of her commander, there is no doubt that ninety-three others would have shared the fate of their companions. Some were Americans and some were British. The excitement in this country was intense, and war with Spain was widely demanded. Further investigation revealed the fact that the American registry was dishonest, that the ship really belonged to or was chartered by Cubans, that it was engaged in carrying supplies and munitions of war to the insurgents, and that its right to fly the American flag was more than doubtful. The ship was seized by the American authorities under a charge of violation of the maritime laws of the United States, and was ordered to New York, for a trial of the case. American naval officers were placed in command, but she was in bad condition, and foundered in a gale near Cape Fear. As far as the vessel was concerned, the incident was closed. There remained the question of indemnity for what Caleb Cushing, then the American Minister to Spain, in his communication to the Spanish authorities, denounced as "a dreadful, a savage act, the inhuman slaughter in cold blood, of fifty-three human beings, a large number of them citizens of the United States, shot without lawful trial, without any valid pretension of authority, and to the horror of the whole civilized world." England also filed its claim for the loss of British subjects, and payment was soon after made "for the purpose of relief of the families or persons of the ship's company and passengers." In his *Cuba and International Relations*, Mr. Callahan says: "The catalogue of irritating affairs in relation to Cuba, of which the *Virginius* was only the culmination, might have been urged as sufficient to justify a policy of intervention to stop the stubborn war of extermination which had been tolerated by peaceful neighbors for five years. Some would have been ready to advocate intervention as a duty. The relations of Cuba to the United States, the Spanish commercial restrictions which placed Cuba at the mercy of Spanish monopolists, and the character of the Spanish rule, pointed to the conclusion that if Spain should not voluntarily grant reforms and guarantee pacification of the island, the United States might be compelled, especially for future security, temporarily to occupy it and assist in the organization of a liberal government based upon modern views. Such action might have led to annexation, but not necessarily; it might have led to a restoration of Spanish possession under restrictions as to the character of Spanish rule, and as to the size of the Spanish army and naval force in the vicinity; more likely it would have resulted in the independence of Cuba under American protection."

These are only some of the more prominent features in fifty years of American interest in Cuba. Throughout the entire period, the sympathies of the

American people were strongly pro-Cuban. Money and supplies were contributed from time to time to assist the Cubans in their efforts to effect a change in their conditions, either through modification of Spanish laws, or by the road of independence. Only a minority of the Cubans sought to follow that road at that time. The movement for independence was not national until it was made so in 1895. What would have happened had we, at the time of the Ten Years' War, granted to the Cubans the rights of belligerents, is altogether a matter of speculation. Such a course was then deemed politically inexpedient.

IX

CUBA'S REVOLUTIONS

Only by magnifying protests into revolts, and riots into revolutions, is it possible to show Cuba as the "land of revolutions" that many have declared it to be. The truth is that from the settlement of the island in 1512 until the signing of the Treaty of Paris in 1898, there were only two experiences that can, by any proper use of the term, be called revolutions. This statement, of course, disputes a widely accepted notion, but many notions become widely accepted because of assertions that are not contradicted. That a strong undercurrent of discontent runs through all Cuba's history from 1820 to 1895, is true. That there were numerous manifestations of that discontent, and occasional attempts at revolution, is also true. But none of these experiences, prior to 1868, reached a stage that would properly warrant its description as a revolution. The term is very loosely applied to a wide range of experiences. It is customary to class as revolution all disorders from riots to rebellions. This is particularly the case where the disorder occurs in some country other than our own. The *Standard Dictionary* defines the essential idea of revolution as "a change in the form of government, or the constitution, or rulers, otherwise than as provided by the laws of succession, election, etc." The *Century Dictionary* defines such proceedings as "a radical change in social or governmental conditions; the overthrow of an established political system." Many exceedingly interesting parallels may be drawn between the experience of the American colonies prior to their revolution, in 1775, and the experience of Cuba during the 19th Century. In fact, it may perhaps be said that there is no experience in Cuba's history that cannot be fairly paralleled in our own. In his *History of the United States*, Mr. Edward Channing says: "The governing classes of the old country wished to exploit the American colonists for their own use and behoof." Change the word "American" to "Spanish," and the Cuban situation is exactly defined. The situation in America in the 18th Century was almost identical with the situation in Cuba in the 19th Century. Both, in those respective periods, suffered from oppressive and restrictive trade laws and from burdensome taxation, from subordination of their interests to the interests of the people of a mother-country three thousand miles away. Unfortunately for the Cubans, Spain was better able to enforce its exactions than England was. Cuba's area was limited, its available harbors few in number, its population small.

Not until the years immediately preceding the revolutions by which the United States and Cuba secured their independence, was there any general demand for definite separation from the mother-country. The desire in both was a fuller measure of economic and commercial opportunity. One striking parallel may be noted. The Tories, or "loyalists," in this country have their counterpart in the Cuban *Autonomistas*. Referring to conditions in 1763, Mr. Channing states that "never had the colonists felt a greater pride in their connection with the British empire." Among the great figures of the pre-revolutionary period in this country, none stands out more clearly than James Otis, of Boston, and Patrick Henry, of Virginia. In an impassioned address, in 1763, Otis declared that "every British subject in America is of common right, by acts of Parliament, and by the laws of God and nature, entitled to all the essential privileges of Britons. What God in his Providence has united let no man dare attempt to pull asunder." Thirteen years later, the sundering blow was struck. Patrick Henry's resolutions submitted to the Virginia House of Burgesses, in 1765, set that colony afire, but at that time neither he nor his associates desired separation and independence if their natural rights were recognized. It was not until the revolution of 1895 that the independence of Cuba became a national demand, a movement based on realization of the hopelessness of further dependence upon Spain for the desired economic and fiscal relief. As in the American colonies there appeared, from time to time, individuals or isolated groups who demanded drastic action on the part of the colonists, so were there Cubans who, from time to time, appeared with similar demands. Nathaniel Bacon headed a formidable revolution in Virginia in 1676. Massachusetts rebelled against Andros and Dudley in 1689. From the passage of the Navigation Acts, in the middle of the 17th Century, until the culmination in 1775, there was an undercurrent of friction and a succession of protests. The Cuban condition was quite the same excepting the fact of burdens more grievous and more frequent open outbreaks.

The records of many of the disorders are fragmentary. Spain had no desire to give them publicity, and the Cubans had few means for doing so. The *Report on the Census of Cuba*, prepared by the War Department of the United States, in 1899, contains a summary of the various disorders in the island. The first is the rioting in 1717, when Captain-General Roja enforced the decree establishing a government monopoly in tobacco. The disturbances in Haiti and Santo Domingo (1791-1800) resulting in the establishment of independence in Haiti, under Toussaint, excited unimportant uprisings on the part of negroes in Cuba, but they were quickly suppressed. The first movement worthy of note came in 1823. It was a consequence of the general movement that extended throughout Spanish-America and resulted in the independence of all Spain's former colonies, excepting Cuba and Porto Rico. That the influence of so vast a movement should have been felt in Cuba was almost inevitable. As disorder continued throughout much of the time, the period 1820-1830 is best considered collectively. The same influences were active, and the same forces were operative for the greater part of the term. The accounts of it all are greatly confused, and several nations were involved, including Spain, the United States, France, England, Mexico, and Colombia. The slavery question was involved, as was the question of the transfer of the island to some Power other than Spain. Independence was the aim of some, though probably no very great number. Practically all of Cuba's later experiences have their roots in this period. During these ten years, the issue between Cubans who sought a larger national and economic life, and the Spanish element that insisted upon the continuance of Spanish absolutism, had its definite beginning, to remain a cause of almost constant friction for three-quarters of a century. The Spanish Constitution of

1812, abrogated in 1814, was again proclaimed in 1820, and again abrogated in 1823. The effort of Captain-General Vives, acting under orders from Ferdinand VII, to restore absolutism encountered both vigorous opposition and strong support. Secret societies were organized, whose exact purposes do not appear to be well known. Some have asserted that it was a Masonic movement, while others have held that the organizations were more in the nature of the *Carbonari*. One of them, called the *Soles de Bolivar*, in some way gave its name to the immediate activities. It was charged with having planned a rebellion against the government, but the plans were discovered and the leaders were arrested. The movement appears to have been widespread, with its headquarters in Matanzas. An uprising was planned to take place on August 16, 1823, but on that day Jose Francisco Lemus, the leader, and a number of his associates were arrested and imprisoned. Among them was José Maria Heredia, the Cuban poet, who was, for this offence, condemned, in 1824, to perpetual exile for the crime of treason.

Others engaged in the conspiracy fled the country. Some were officially deported. But the punishments imposed on these people served to excite the animosity of many more, and a period of agitation followed, marked by occasional outbreaks and rioting. To meet the situation, an army intended to be employed in reconquering some of the colonies that had already declared and established their independence, was retained on the island. In 1825, a royal decree conferred on the Spanish Governor in Cuba a power practically absolute. This excited still further the anger of the Cuban element and led to other manifestations of discontent. There was a combination of political agitation with revolutionary demonstrations. In 1826, there was a local uprising in Puerto Principe, directed more particularly against the Spanish garrison, whose conduct was regarded as highly offensive. A year or two later, Cuban exiles in Mexico and Colombia, with support from the people of those countries, organized a secret society known as the "Black Eagle," having for its purpose a Cuban revolution. Its headquarters were in Mexico, and its activities were fruitless. Many were arrested and tried and sentenced to death or deportation. But Vives realized the folly of adding more fuel to the flames, and the sentences were in all cases either mitigated or revoked. This seems to have brought that particular series of conspiracies to an end. It was a time of active political agitation and conspiracy, with occasional local riots that were quickly suppressed. While much of it was revolutionary in its aims and purposes, none of it may with any fitness be called a revolution, unless a prevalence of a lively spirit of opposition and rebellion is to be so classed. The agitation settled down for a number of years, but broke out in local spasms occasionally. There were riots and disorders, but that is not revolution. It is to be remembered that the cause of all this disturbance was, in the main, an entirely creditable sentiment, quite as creditable as that which led the American colonists to resist the Stamp taxes and to destroy tea. It was a natural and righteous protest against oppression, a movement lasting for seventy-five years, for which Americans, particularly, should award praise rather than blame or carping criticism. Having done, in our own way, very much what the Cubans have done, in their way, we are not free to condemn them. The only real difference is that their methods were, on the whole, a little more strenuous than ours. Cuban blood was stirred by the successful revolutions in Mexico and in Spanish South America, and conditions in the island were contrasted with those in the then somewhat new United States. Something of the part played by this country in the experiences of the time is presented in another chapter, on the relations of the two countries.

The next movement worthy of note came in 1849, if we omit the quarrel, in 1837, between General Tacon and his subordinate, General Lorenzo, and the alleged proposal of the slaves in the neighborhood of Matanzas to rise and slaughter all the whites. Neither of these quite belongs in the revolutionary class. In 1847, a conspiracy was organized in the vicinity of Cienfuegos. Its leader was General Narciso Lopez. The movement was discovered, and some of the participants were imprisoned. Lopez escaped to the United States where he associated himself with a group of Cuban exiles, and opened correspondence with sympathizers in the island. They were joined by a considerable number of adventurous Americans, inspired by a variety of motives. The declared purpose of the enterprise was independence as the alternative of reform in Spanish laws. An expedition was organized, but the plans became known and President Taylor, on August 11, 1849, issued a proclamation in which he declared that "an enterprise to invade the territories of a friendly nation, set on foot and prosecuted within the limits of the United States, is in the highest degree criminal." He therefore warned all citizens of the United States who might participate in such an enterprise that they would be subject to heavy penalties, and would forfeit the protection of their country. He also called on "every officer of this Government, civil or military, to use all efforts in his power to arrest for trial and punishment every such offender against the laws." The party was captured as it was leaving New York. The best evidence of the time is to the effect that there was in Cuba neither demand for nor support of such a movement, but Lopez and his associates, many of them Americans, persisted. A second expedition was arranged, and a party of more than six hundred men, many of them American citizens, assembled on the island of Contoy, off the Yucatan coast, and on May 19, 1850, landed at Cardenas. But there was no uprising on the part of the people. The Spanish authorities, informed of the expedition, sent ships by sea and troops by land. After a sharp skirmish, the invaders fled for their lives. Lopez and those who escaped with him succeeded in reaching Key West. He went to Savannah, where he was arrested but promptly liberated in response to public clamor. But even this did not satisfy the enthusiastic liberator of a people who did not want to be liberated in that way. He tried again in the following year. On August 3, 1851, he sailed from near New Orleans, on the steamer *Pampero*, in command of a force of about four hundred, largely composed of young Americans who had been lured into the enterprise by assurance of thrilling adventure and large pay. They landed near Bahia Honda, about fifty miles west of Havana. Here, again, the Cubans refused to rise and join the invaders. Here, again, they encountered the Spanish forces by whom they were beaten and routed. Many were killed, some were captured, and others escaped into the surrounding country and were captured afterward. Lopez was among the captured. He was taken to Havana, and died by *garrote* in the little fortress La Punta. His first officer, Colonel Crittenden, and some fifty Americans were captured and taken to Atares, the fortress at the head of Havana harbor, where they were shot. For that somewhat brutal act, the United States could ask no indemnity. In violation of the laws of the United States, they had invaded the territory of a nation with which the country was at peace. In the initial issue of the *New York Times*, on October 18, 1851, there appeared a review of the incident, presenting a contemporaneous opinion of the experience. It was, in part, as follows:

"Nothing can be clearer than the fact that, for the present, at least, the inhabitants of Cuba do not desire their freedom. The opinion has very widely prevailed that the Cubans were grievously oppressed by their Spanish rulers, and that the severity of their oppression alone prevented them from making some effort to throw it off. The presence of an armed force in their midst, however small, it was supposed would summon them by thousands to the standard of revolt, and convert the colony into a free republic. Men high in office, men who had lived in Cuba and were supposed to be familiar with the sentiments of its people, have uniformly represented that they were ripe for revolt, and desired only the presence of a small military band to serve as a nucleus for their force. Believing that the Cuban population would aid them, American adventurers enlisted and were ruined. They found no aid. Not a Cuban joined them. They were treated as pirates and robbers from the first moment of their landing. Nor could they expect any other treatment in case of failure. They ceased to be American citizens the moment they set out, as invaders, for the shores of Cuba."

The excitement of the Lopez incident was passing when it was revived, in 1854, by the *Black Warrior* experience, to which reference is made elsewhere. Another invasion was projected by exuberant and adventurous Americans. It was to sail from New Orleans under command of General Quitman, a former Governor of the State of Mississippi. No secret was made of the expedition, and Quitman openly boasted of his purposes, in Washington. The reports having reached the White House, President Pierce issued a proclamation warning "all persons, citizens of the United States and others residing therein" that the General Government would not fail to prosecute with due energy all those who presumed to disregard the laws of the land and our treaty obligations. He charged all officers of the United States to exert all their lawful power to maintain the authority and preserve the peace of the country. Quitman was arrested, and put under bonds to respect the neutrality laws. There was a limited uprising in Puerto Principe, in 1851, and a conspiracy was revealed, in Pinar del Rio, in 1852. A few years later the Liberal Club in Havana and the Cuban Junta in New York were reported as raising money and organizing expeditions. Some sailed, but they accomplished little, except as the activities appear as a manifestation of the persistent opposition on the part of what was probably only a small minority of the Cuban people. For several years, the unrest and the agitation continued. Spain's blindness to the situation is puzzling. In his *Cuba and*

International Relations, Mr. Callahan says: "Spain, after squandering a continent, had still clung tenaciously to Cuba; and the changing governments which had been born (in Spain) only to be strangled, held her with a taxing hand. While England had allowed her colonies to rule themselves, Spain had persisted in keeping Cuba in the same state of tutelage that existed when she was the greatest power in the world, and when the idea of colonial rights had not developed." In *Tomorrow in Cuba*, Mr. Pepper notes that "though the conception of colonial home rule for Cuba was non-existent among the Spanish statesmen of that day, the perception of it was clear on the part of the thinking people of the island. The educated and wealthy Cubans who in 1865 formed themselves into a national party and urged administrative and economic changes upon Madrid felt the lack of understanding among Spanish statesmen. The concessions asked were not a broad application of civil liberties. When their programme was rejected in its entirety they ceased to ask favors. They inaugurated the Ten Years' War." Regarding this action by the Cubans, Dr. Enrique José Varona, a distinguished Cuban and a former deputy to the Cortes, has stated that "before the insurrection of 1868, the reform party which included the most enlightened, wealthy, and influential Cubans, exhausted all the resources within their reach to induce Spain to initiate a healthy change in her Cuban policy. The party started the publication of periodicals in Madrid and in the island, addressed petitions, maintained a great agitation throughout the country, and having succeeded in leading the Spanish Government to make an inquiry into the economic, political, and social conditions in Cuba, they presented a complete plan of government which satisfied public requirements as well as the aspirations of the people. The Spanish Government disdainfully cast aside the proposition as useless, increased taxation, and proceeded to its exaction with extreme severity." Here not seek its independence; the object was reform in oppressive laws and in burdensome taxation, a measure of self-government, under Spain, and a greater industrial and commercial freedom. It is most difficult to understand the short-sightedness of the Spanish authorities. The war soon followed the refusal of these entirely reasonable demands, and the course of the Cubans is entirely to their credit. An acceptance of the situation and a further submission would have shown them as contemptible.

The details of a conflict that lasted for ten years are quite impossible of presentation in a few pages. Nor are they of value or interest to any except special students who can find them elaborately set forth in many volumes, some in Spanish and a few in English. Having tried once before to cover this period as briefly and as adequately as possible, I can do no better here than to repeat the story as told in an earlier work (*Cuba, and the Intervention*). On the 10th of October, 1868, Carlos Manuel Cespedes and his associates raised the cry of Cuban independence at Yara, in the Province of Puerto Principe (now Camaguey). On the 10th of April, 1869, there was proclaimed the Constitution of the Cuban Republic. During the intervening months, there was considerable fighting, though it was largely in the nature of guerrilla skirmishing. The Spanish Minister of State asserted in a memorandum issued to Spain's representatives in other countries, under date of February 3, 1876, that at the outbreak of the insurrection Spain had 7,500 troops, all told, in Cuba. According to General Sickels, at that time the American Minister to Spain, this number was increased by reinforcements of 34,500 within the first year of the war. The accuracy of this information, however, has been questioned. Prior to the establishment of the so-called Republic, the affairs of the insurrection were in the hands of an Assembly of Representatives. On February 26, this body issued a decree proclaiming the abolition of slavery throughout the island, and calling upon those who thus received their freedom to "contribute their efforts to the independence of Cuba." During the opening days of April, 1869, the Assembly met at Guiamaro. On the tenth of that month a government was organized, with a president, vice-president, general-in-chief of the army, secretaries of departments, and a parliament or congress. Carlos Manuel Cespedes was chosen as President, and Manuel de Quesada as General-in-Chief. A Constitution was adopted. Señor Morales Lemus was appointed as minister to the United States, to represent the new Republic, and to ask official recognition by the American Government. The government which the United States was asked to recognize was a somewhat vague institution. The insurrection, or revolution, if it may be so called, at this time consisted of a nominal central government, chiefly self-organized and self-elected, and various roving bands, probably numbering some thousands in their aggregate, of men rudely and incompetently armed, and showing little or nothing of military organization or method.

Like all Cuban-Spanish wars and warfare, the destruction of property was a common procedure. Some of the methods employed for the suppression of the insurrection were not unlike those adopted by General Weyler in the later war. At Bayamo, on April 4, 1869, Count Valmaseda, the Spanish Commandant of that district, issued the following proclamation:

1. Every man, from the age of fifteen years upward, found away from his place of habitation, who does not prove a justified reason therefor, will be shot.
2. Every unoccupied habitation will be burned by the troops.
3. Every habitation from which no white flag floats, as a signal that its occupants desire peace, will be reduced to ashes.

In the summer of 1869, the United States essayed a reconciliation and an adjustment of the differences between the contestants. To this Spain replied that the mediation of any nation in a purely domestic question was wholly incompatible with the honor of Spain, and that the independence of Cuba was inadmissible as a basis of negotiation. Heavy reinforcements were sent from Spain, and the strife continued. The commerce of the island was not greatly disturbed, for the reason that the great producing and commercial centres lay to the westward, and the military activities were confined, almost exclusively, to the eastern and central areas. In April, 1874, Mr. Fish, then Secretary of State, reported that "it is now more than five years since the uprising (in Cuba) and it has been announced with apparent authority, that Spain has lost upward of 80,000 men, and has expended upward of $100,000,000, in efforts to suppress it; yet the insurrection seems today as active and as powerful as it has ever been." Spain's losses among her troops were not due so much to the casualties of war as they were to the ravages of disease, especially yellow fever. The process, in which both parties would appear to be about equally culpable, of destroying property and taking life when occasion offered, proceedings which are hardly to be dignified by the name of war, continued until the beginning of 1878. Throughout the entire period of the war, the American officials labored diligently for its termination on a basis that would give fair promise of an enduring peace. Many questions arose concerning the arrest of American citizens and the destruction of property of American ownership. Proposals to grant the Cubans the rights of belligerents were dismissed as not properly warranted by the conditions, and questions arose regarding the supply of arms and ammunition, from this country, by filibustering expeditions. References to Cuban affairs appear in many presidential messages, and the matter was a subject of much discussion and numerous measures in Congress. Diplomatic communication was constantly active. In his message of December 7, 1875, President Grant said: "The past year has furnished no evidence of an approaching termination of the ruinous conflict which has been raging for seven years in the neighboring island of Cuba. While conscious that the insurrection has shown a strength and endurance which make it at least doubtful whether it be in the power of Spain to subdue it, it seems unquestionable that no such civil organization exists which may be recognized as an independent government capable of performing its international obligations and entitled to be treated as one of the powers of the earth." Nor did he then deem the grant of belligerent rights to the Cubans as either expedient or properly warranted by the circumstances.

In 1878, Martinez Campos was Governor-General of Cuba, and Maximo Gomez was Commander-in-Chief of the Cuban forces. Both parties were weary of the prolonged hostilities, and neither was able to compel the other to surrender. Spain, however, professed a willingness to yield an important part of the demands of her rebellious subjects. Martinez Campos and Gomez met at Zanjon and, on February 10, 1878, mutually agreed to what has been variously called a peace pact, a treaty, and a capitulation. The agreement was based on provisions for a redress of Cuban grievances through greater civil, political, and administrative privileges for the Cubans, with forgetfulness of the past and amnesty for all then under sentence for political offences. Delay in carrying these provisions into effect gave rise to an attempt to renew the struggle two years later, but the effort was a failure.

Matters then quieted down for a number of years. The Cubans waited to see what would be done. The Spanish Governor-General still remained the supreme power and, aside from the abolition of slavery, the application of the Spanish Constitution and Spanish laws to Cuba, and Cuban representation in the Cortes, much of which was rather form than fact, the island gained little by the new conditions. Discontent and protest continued and, at last, broke again into open rebellion in 1895.

The story of that experience is told in another chapter. In 1906, there came one of the most deplorable experiences in the history of the island, the first and only discreditable revolution. The causes of the experience are not open to our criticism. Our own records show too much of precisely the same kind of work, illegal registration, ballot box stuffing, threats and bribery. The first election in the new Republic was carried with only a limited and somewhat perfunctory opposition to the candidacy of Estrada Palma. Before the second election came, in 1905, he allied himself definitely with an organization then known as the Moderate party. The opposition was known as the Liberal party. Responsibility for the disgraceful campaign that followed rests on both, almost equally. The particular difference lies in the fact that, the principal offices having been given to adherents of the Moderates, they were able to control both registration and election proceedings. But the methods employed by the opposition were no less censurable. Realizing defeat, the Liberals withdrew from the field, by concerted action, on the day of the election, and the Moderates elected every one of their candidates. Naturally, a feeling of bitter resentment was created, and there came, in the spring of 1906, rumors of armed revolt. In August, an actual insurrection was begun. Disgruntled political leaders gathered formidable bands in Pinar del Rio and in Santa Clara provinces. President Palma became seriously alarmed, even actually frightened. Through the United States Consul-General in Havana, he sent urgent appeals to Washington for naval and military aid. Mr. Taft, then Secretary of War, and Mr. Bacon, the Assistant Secretary of State, were sent to Havana to investigate and report on the situation. They arrived in Havana on September 19. After ten days of careful and thorough study, and earnest effort to effect an adjustment, a proclamation was issued declaring the creation of a provisional government. This was accepted by both parties and the insurgent bands dispersed. Charles E. Magoon was sent down as Provisional Governor. Americans who are disposed to censure the Cubans for this experience in their history, may perhaps turn with profit to some little experiences in the history of their own country in its political infancy, in 1786 and 1794. Those incidents do not relieve the Cubans of the censure to which they are open, but they make it a little difficult for us to condemn them with proper grace and dignity. The provisional government continued until January 28, 1909, when control was turned over to the duly elected officials, they being the same who withdrew from the polls, acknowledging defeat, in the election of 1905.

X

INDEPENDENCE

Cuba's final movement for independence began on February 24, 1895. Under the treaty of Zanjon, executed in 1878, Spain agreed to grant to the Cubans such reforms as would remove their grounds of complaint, long continued. The Cubans denied that the terms of the agreement had been kept. Those terms are indicated in a statement submitted by Tomas Estrada y Palma to Richard Olney, then Secretary of State of the United States. It bore the date of December 7, 1895. The communication sets forth, from the Cuban point of view, of course, the causes of the revolution of 1895. It says:

"These causes are substantially the same as those of the former revolution, lasting from 1868 to 1878, and terminating only on the representation of the Spanish Government that Cuba would be granted such reforms as would remove the grounds of complaint on the part of the Cuban people. Unfortunately the hopes thus held out have never been realized. The representation which was to be given the Cubans has proved to be absolutely without character; taxes have been levied anew on everything conceivable; the offices in the island have increased, but the officers are all Spaniards; the native Cubans have been left with no public duties whatsoever to perform, except the payment of taxes to the Government and blackmail to the officials, without privilege even to move from place to place in the island except on the permission of government authority.

"Spain has framed laws so that the natives have substantially been deprived of the right of suffrage. The taxes levied have been almost entirely devoted to support the army and navy in Cuba, to pay interest on the debt that Spain has saddled on the island, and to pay the salaries of the vast number of Spanish office holders, devoting only $746,000 for internal improvements out of the $26,000,000 collected by tax. No public schools are in reach of the masses for their education. All the principal industries of the island are hampered by excessive imposts. Her commerce with every country but Spain has been crippled in every possible manner, as can readily be seen by the frequent protests of shipowners and merchants.

"The Cubans have no security of person or property. The judiciary are instruments of the military authorities. Trial by military tribunals can be ordered at any time at the will of the Captain-General. There is, besides, no freedom of speech, press, or religion. In point of fact, the causes of the Revolution of 1775 in this country were not nearly as grave as those that have driven the Cuban people to the various insurrections which culminated in the present revolution."

Spain, of course, denied these charges, and asserted that the agreement had been kept in good faith. The Spanish Government may have been technically correct in its claim that all laws necessary to the fulfillment of its promises had been enacted. But it seems entirely certain that they had not been made effective. The conditions of the Cubans were in no way improved and, some time before the outbreak, they began preparations for armed resistance. In *Cuba and the Intervention* (published in 1905) I have already written an outline review of the experience of the revolution, and I shall here make use of extracts from that volume. The notable leader and instigator of the movement was José Marti, a patriot, a poet, and a dreamer, but a man of action. He visited General Maximo Gomez at his home in Santo Domingo, where that doughty old warrior had betaken himself after the conclusion of the Ten Years' War. Gomez accepted the command of the proposed army of Cuban liberation. Antonio Maceo also accepted a command. He was a mulatto, an able and daring fighter, whose motives were perhaps a compound of patriotism, hatred of Spain, and a love for the excitement of warfare. Others whose names are written large in Cuba's history soon joined the movement. A *junta*, or committee, was organized with headquarters in New York. After the death of Marti, this was placed in charge of Tomas Estrada y Palma, who afterward became the first President of the new Republic. Its work was to raise funds, obtain and forward supplies and ammunition, and to advance the cause in all possible ways. There were legal battles to be fought by and through this organization, and Mr. Horatio S. Rubens, a New York lawyer, was placed in charge of that department. The twenty-fourth of February was set for the beginning of activities, but arms were lacking, and while the movement was actually begun on that day, the operations of the first six weeks or so were limited to numerous local uprisings of little moment. But the local authorities became alarmed, and martial law was proclaimed in Santa Clara and Matanzas provinces on the 27th. Spain became alarmed also, and immediately despatched General Martinez Campos as Governor-General of the island, to succeed General Calleja. He assumed command on April 16. Maceo and his associates, among them his brother José, also a fighter of note, landed from Costa Rica on April 1. Marti, Gomez, and others, reached the island on the 11th. Meanwhile, Bartolomé Maso, an influential planter in Oriente, had been in command of the forces in his vicinity. Many joined, and others stood ready to join as soon as they could be equipped. Engagements with the Spanish troops soon became a matter of daily occurrence, and Martinez Campos realized that a formidable movement was on. Spain hurried thousands of soldiers to the island.

For the first five months, the insurgents kept their opponents busy with an almost uninterrupted series of little engagements, a guerrilla warfare. In one of these, on May 19, José Marti was killed. His death was a severe blow to the patriots, but it served rather to inspire a greater activity than to check the movement. His death came in the effort of a small band of insurgents to pass the Spanish cordon designed to confine activities to Oriente Province. Immediately after the death of Marti, Maximo Gomez crossed that barrier and organized an army in Camaguey. The first engagement properly to be regarded as a battle occurred at Peralejo, near Bayamo, in Oriente, about the middle of July. The respective leaders were Antonio Maceo and General Martinez Campos, in person. The victory fell to Maceo, and Martinez Campos barely eluded capture. The engagements of the Ten Years' War were confined to the then sparsely settled eastern half of the island. Those of the revolution of 1895 covered the greater part of the island, sweeping gradually but steadily from east to west. During my first visit to Cuba, I was frequently puzzled by references to "the invasion." "What invasion?" I asked, "Who invaded the country?" I found that it meant the westward sweep of the liberating army under Gomez and Maceo. It covered a period of more than two years of frequent fighting and general destruction of property. Early in the operations Gomez issued the following proclamation:

GENERAL HEADQUARTERS OF THE ARMY OF LIBERATION
Najasa, Camaguey, July 1, 1895.

To THE PLANTERS AND OWNERS OF CATTLE RANCHES:
In accord with the great interests of the revolution for the independence of the country, and for which we are in arms:

WHEREAS, *all exploitations of any product whatsoever are aids and resources to the Government that we are fighting, it is resolved by the general-in-chief to issue this general order throughout the island, that the introduction of articles of commerce, as well as beef and cattle, into the towns occupied by the enemy, is absolutely prohibited. The sugar plantations will stop their labors, and those who shall attempt to grind the crop notwithstanding this order, will have their cane burned and their buildings demolished. The person who, disobeying this order, shall try to profit from the present situation of affairs, will show by his conduct little respect for the rights of the revolution of redemption, and therefore shall be considered as an enemy, treated as a traitor, and tried as such in case of his capture.*

(*Signed*) MAXIMO GOMEZ,
The General-in-Chief.

This proved only partially effective, and it was followed by a circular to commanding officers, a few months later, reading thus:

HEADQUARTERS OF THE ARMY OF LIBERATION
Territory of Sancti Spiritus, November 6, 1895.

Animated by the spirit of unchangeable resolution in defence of the rights of the revolution of redemption of this country of colonists, humiliated and despised by Spain, and in harmony with what has been decreed concerning the subject in the circular dated the 1st of July, I have ordered the following:

ARTICLE I. *That all plantations shall be totally destroyed, their cane and outbuildings burned, and railroad connections destroyed.*

ARTICLE II. *All laborers who shall aid the sugar factories—these sources of supplies that we must deprive the enemy of—shall be considered as traitors to their country.*

ARTICLE III. *All who are caught in the act, or whose violation of Article II shall be proven, shall be shot. Let all chiefs of operations of the army of liberty comply with this order, determined to furl triumphantly, even over ruin and ashes, the flag of the Republic of Cuba.*

In regard to the manner of waging the war, follow the private instructions that I have already given.

For the sake of the honor of our arms and your well-known courage and patriotism, it is expected that you will strictly comply with the above orders.

(Signed) MAXIMO GOMEZ,
General-in-Chief.

To peace-loving souls, all this sounds very brutal, but all war is brutal and barbarous. In our strife in the Philippines, from 1899 to 1902, many of us were proud to be told that we were conducting a "humane war." There is no such thing. The very terms are contradictory. Gomez had declared that if Spain would not give up Cuba to the Cubans, the Cubans would themselves render the island so worthless and desolate a possession that Spain could not afford to hold it. Short of further submission to a rule that was, very rightly, regarded as no longer endurable, no other course was open to them. Another proclamation appeared a few days later.

HEADQUARTERS OF THE ARMY OF
LIBERATION
Sancti Spiritus, November 11 1895.

To HONEST MEN, VICTIMS OF THE TORCH:
The painful measure made necessary by the revolution of redemption drenched in innocent blood from Hatuey to our own times by cruel and merciless Spain will plunge you in misery. As general-in-chief of the army of liberation, it is my duty to lead it to victory, without permitting myself to be restrained or terrified, by any means necessary to place Cuba in the shortest time in possession of her dearest ideal. I therefore place the responsibility for so great a ruin on those who look on impassively and force us to those extreme measures which they then condemn like dolts and hypocrites as they are. After so many years of supplication, humiliation, contumely, banishment, and death, when this people, of its own will, has arisen in arms, there remains no solution but to triumph, it matters not what means are employed to accomplish it.

This people cannot hesitate between the wealth of Spain and the liberty of Cuba. Its greatest crime would be to stain the land with blood without effecting its purposes because of puerile scruples and fears which do not concur with the character of the men who are in the field, challenging the fury of an army which is one of the bravest in the world, but which in this war is without enthusiasm or faith, ill-fed and unpaid. The war did not begin February 24; it is about to begin now.
The war had to be organized; it was necessary to calm and lead into the proper channels the revolutionary spirit always exaggerated in the beginning by wild enthusiasm. The struggle ought to begin in obedience to a plan and method more or less studied, as the result of the peculiarities of this war. This has already been done. Let Spain now send her soldiers to rivet the chains on her slaves; the children of this land are in the field, armed with the weapons of liberty. The struggle will be terrible, but success will crown the revolution and the efforts of the oppressed.

(*Signed*) MAXIMO GOMEZ,
General-in-Chief.

Such an address doubtless savors of bombast to many Americans, but in the history of political and military oratory in their own land they can find an endless number of speeches that, in that particular quality, rival if they do not surpass it. The Cuban situation was desperate, and the Cuban attitude was one of fixed determination. Productive industry was generally suppressed, and much property was destroyed, by both Cubans and Spaniards. This necessarily threw many out of employment, and drove them into the insurgent ranks. The Cubans are a peaceful people. All desired relief from oppressive conditions, but many did not want war. While many entered the army from patriotic motives, many others were brought into it only as a consequence of conditions created by the conflict. The measures adopted were severe, but decision of the contest by pitched battles was quite impossible. The quoted figures are somewhat unreliable, but the Spanish forces outnumbered the Cubans by at least five to one, and they could obtain freely the supplies and ammunition that the Cubans could obtain only by filibustering expeditions. The Cubans, therefore, adopted a policy, the only policy that afforded promise of success. Spain poured in fresh troops until, by the close of 1895, its army is reported as numbering 200,000 men.

The Cubans carried the contest westward from Oriente and Camaguey, through Santa Clara, and into the provinces of Matanzas, Havana, and Pinar del Rio.

The *trocha* across the island, from Jucaro on the south to Moron on the north, originally constructed during the Ten Years' War, was a line of blockhouses, connected by barbed wire tangles, along a railway. This obstructed but did not stop the Cuban advance. The authorities declared martial law in the provinces of Havana and Pinar del Rio on January 2, 1896. Gomez advanced to Marianao, at Havana's very door, and that city was terrified. Maceo was operating immediately beyond him in Pinar del Rio, through the most important part of which he swept with torch and machete. The Spaniards built a *trocha* there from Mariel southward. Maceo crossed it and continued his work of destruction, in which large numbers of the people of the region joined. He burned and destroyed Spanish property; the Spaniards, in retaliation, burned and destroyed property belonging to Cubans. Along the highway from Marianao to Guanajay, out of many stately country residences, only one was left standing. Villages were destroyed and hamlets were wrecked. On one of his expeditions in December, 1896, Maceo was killed near Punta Brava, within fifteen miles of Havana. Gomez planned this westward sweep, from Oriente, six hundred miles away, but to Antonio Maceo belongs a large part of the credit for its execution. The weakness of the Ten Years' War was that it did not extend beyond the thinly populated region of the east; Gomez and Maceo carried their war to the very gates of the Spanish strongholds. There were occasional conflicts that might well be called battles, but much of it was carried on by the Cubans by sudden and unexpected dashes into Spanish camps or moving columns, brief but sometimes bloody encounters from which the attacking force melted away after inflicting such damage as it could. Guerrilla warfare is not perhaps a respectable method of fighting. It involves much of what is commonly regarded as outlawry, of pillage and of plunder, of destruction and devastation. These results become respectable only when attained through conventional processes, and are in some way supposed to be ennobled by those processes. But they sometimes become the only means by which the weak can meet the strong. Such they seemed to be in the Cuban revolt against the Spaniards, when Maximo Gomez and Antonio Maceo made guerrilla warfare almost a military science. Gomez formulated his plan of campaign, but, with the means at his disposal, its successful execution was possible only by the methods adopted. At all events, it succeeded. The Cubans were not strong enough to drive Spain out of the island by force of arms, but they showed themselves unconquerable by the Spanish troops. They had once carried on a war for ten years in a limited area; by the methods adopted, they could repeat that experience practically throughout the island. They could at least keep insurrection alive until Spain should yield to their terms, or until the United States should be compelled to intervene. No great movements, but constant irritation, and the suspension of all industry, was the policy adopted and pursued for the year 1897.

But there was another side to it all, a different line of activity. Immediately after his arrival on the island, on April 11, 1895, Marti had issued a call for the selection of representatives to form a civil government. He was killed before this was effected. An assembly met, at Jimaguayu, in Camaguey, on September 13, 1895. It consisted of twenty members, representing nearly all parts of the island. Its purpose was the organization of a Cuban Republic. On the 16th, it adopted a Constitution and, on the 18th, elected, as President, Salvador Cisneros Betancourt, and as Vice-President, Bartolomé Maso. Secretaries and sub-secretaries were duly chosen, and all were formally installed. Maximo Gomez was officially appointed as General-in-Chief of the army, with Antonio Maceo as Lieutenant General. Tomas Estrada y Palma was chosen as delegate plenipotentiary and general agent abroad, with headquarters in New York. Both civil and military organizations were, for a time, crude and somewhat incoherent. It could not be otherwise. They were engaged in a movement that could only succeed by success. Arms and money were lacking. The civil government was desirable in a field that the military arm could not cover. Action lay with the military and with the Cuban Junta in the United States. The latter organization immediately became active. Calls were made for financial assistance and liberal responses were made, chiefly by Cubans. In 1896 and 1897, bonds were issued and sold, or were exchanged for supplies and munitions of war. For a number of years scandalous stories were afloat declaring that these bonds were printed by the acre, and issued, purely for speculative purposes, to the extent of millions upon millions of dollars. The truth is that every bond printed, whether issued or unissued, has been fully accounted for, the actual issue being about $2,200,000. Provision was made in Cuba's Constitution for the recognition of this indebtedness, and it has since been discharged, while the plates and the unused bonds have been destroyed. There may have been speculation in the bonds, as there was in the bonds issued by the United States during the Civil War, but Cuba's conduct in the whole matter has been honest and most honorable. In that matter certainly, its detractors have been confounded. The principal difficulty encountered by the *junta* was the despatch to Cuba of the men and the munitions so greatly needed by those in the field. That, however, is a story that I shall endeavor to tell, in part, in another chapter. It cannot now, if ever, be told in full.

Meanwhile, a complicated political situation developed. The story is too long and too complicated for review in detail. It may be given in general outline. The Peace of 1878 was followed by the organization of political parties, the Liberal and the Union Constitutional. At first, there was comparatively little difference in the essence of their respective platforms, but the lines diverged as the situation developed. The Liberal party became, and remained, the Cuban party, and the Union Constitutional became the Spanish party. Later on, the Liberals became the Autonomists. Their object, for twenty years, was reform in conditions under the rule of Spain. There was no independence party. That was organized, in 1895, by Marti, Gomez, Maceo, Maso, and their associates. It had only one plank in its platform—*Cuba Libre y Independiente*—whatever the cost to the island and its people. "The Autonomist group," says Mr. Pepper, in his *Tomorrow in Cuba*, "became as much a political party as it could become under Spanish institutions." It grew in strength and influence, and continued its agitation persistently and stubbornly. The Spanish Cortes busied itself with discussion of Cuban affairs, but reached no conclusions, produced no results. In 1893, there came the definite organization of the Reformist party, with aims not differing greatly from those of the *Autonomistas*. But Spain delayed until Marti and his followers struck their blow. Official efforts to placate them failed utterly, as did efforts to intimidate them or to conquer them. The Autonomists declared their support of the existing Government, and rebuked the insurgents in a *manifesto* issued on April 4, 1895, six weeks after the outbreak. They only succeeded in antagonizing both sides, the Spanish authorities and the revolutionists. Spain, greatly alarmed, recalled Martinez Campos and sent out Weyler to succeed him. Had Spain followed the advice of Martinez Campos, the failure of the insurrection would have been little short of certain. It sent out Weyler, on whom the Cubans, twenty years earlier, had conferred the title of "Butcher." This step threw to the side of the insurgents the great mass of the middle class Cubans who had previously wavered in uncertainty, questioning the success of revolution while adhering to its general object. Weyler instituted the brutal policy that came to be known as reconcentration. It may be said, in a way, that the Cuban forces themselves instituted this policy. To clear the country in which they were operating, they had ordered all Spaniards and Spanish sympathizers to betake themselves to the cities and towns occupied by Spanish garrisons. This was inconvenient for its victims, but its purpose was humane. Gomez also sought to concentrate the Cubans, particularly the women and children, in the recesses of the hills where they would be less exposed to danger than they would be in their homes. This also was a humane purpose.

Weyler's application of this policy was utterly brutal. The people of the country were herded in prison camps, in settlements surrounded by stockades or trenches beyond which they might not pass. No provision was made for their food or maintenance. The victims were non-combatants, women, and children. In his message of December, 1897, President McKinley said of this system, as applied by Weyler, "It was not civilized warfare; it was extermination. The only peace it could beget was that of the wilderness and the grave." In my experience as a campaign correspondent in several conflicts, I have necessarily seen more or less of gruesome sights, the result of disease and wounds, but I have seen nothing in any way comparable, in horror and pitifulness, to the victims of this abominable system. To describe their condition in detail would be little short of offensive, those groups of hopeless, helpless sufferers who lingered only until death came and kindly put them out of their misery and pain. But by this time, two forces had come into active operation, dire alarm in Spain and wrath and indignation in the United States. Weyler had failed as Martinez Campos, when leaving the island, predicted. He was recalled, and was succeeded, on October 31, 1897, by General Blanco. The new incumbent tried conciliation, but it failed. The work had gone too far. The party in the field had become the dominant party, not to be suppressed either by force of arms or by promises of political and economic reform. At last, Spain yielded. Outside pressure on Madrid, chiefly from the United States, prevailed. A scheme for Cuban autonomy was devised and, on January 1, 1898, was put into effect. But it came too late. It was welcomed by many non-participants in the war, and a form of government was organized under it. But the party then dominant, the army in the field, distrusted the arrangement and would have none of it. All overtures were rejected and the struggle continued. On February 15, 1898, came the disaster to the battleship *Maine*, in the harbor of Havana. On April 11th, President McKinley's historic message went to Congress, declaring that "the only hope of relief and repose from a condition which can no longer be endured is the enforced pacification of Cuba," and asking for power and authority to use the military and naval forces of the United States to effect a termination of the strife in Cuba. Such, in the briefest possible outline, is the record of this eventful period, eventful alike for Cuba and for the United States.

During this struggle, the people of the United States became deeply interested in the affairs of the island, and the Administration in Washington became gravely concerned by them. A preceding chapter, on the United States and Cuba, dropped the matter of the relations of this country to the island at the end of the Ten Years' War, but the relations were by no means dropped, nor were they even suspended. The affairs of the island appear again and again in diplomatic correspondence and in presidential messages. The platform of the Republican party, adopted at the national convention in St. Louis, on June 18, 1896, contained the following: "From the hour of achieving their own independence, the people of the United States have regarded with sympathy the struggles of other American peoples to free themselves from European domination. We watch with deep and abiding interest the heroic battle of the Cuban patriots against cruelty and oppression, and our best hopes go out for the full success of their determined contest for liberty. The Government of Spain having lost control of Cuba and being unable to protect the property or lives of resident American citizens, or to comply with its treaty obligations, we believe that the Government of the United States should actively use its influence and good offices to restore peace and give independence to the island." The Democratic party platform of the same year stated that "we extend our sympathy to the people of Cuba in their heroic struggle for liberty and independence." The platform of the People's party likewise expressed sympathy, and declared the belief that the time had come when "the United States should recognize that Cuba is and of right ought to be a free and independent State." This may be regarded as the almost unanimous opinion of the people of this country at that time. In 1896 and 1897 many resolutions were introduced in the Congress urging action for the recognition of Cuban independence. There was frequent and prolonged debate on the question, but no final action was taken. In his message of December, 1897, President McKinley said: "Of the untried measures (regarding Cuba) there remain only: Recognition of the insurgents as belligerents; recognition of the independence of Cuba; neutral intervention to end the war by imposing a rational compromise between the contestants; and intervention in favor of one or the other party. I speak not of forcible annexation, for that cannot be thought of. That, by our code of morality, would be criminal aggression."

Recognition of the Cubans as belligerents would have effected a radical change in the situation. It would have given the Cubans the right to buy in the American market the arms and supplies that they could then only obtain surreptitiously, that they could only ship by "filibustering expeditions," by blockade-runners. In law, the propriety of granting belligerent rights depends upon the establishment of certain facts, upon the proof of the existence of certain conditions. Those conditions did then exist in Cuba. An unanswerable argument was submitted by Horatio S. Rubens, Esq., the able counsel of the Cuban *junta* in New York. The Cubans never asked for intervention by the United States; they did, with full justification, ask for recognition as belligerents. The consent of this country was deemed inexpedient on political rather than on moral grounds. Had it suited the purposes of this country to grant that right, very much the same arguments would have been made in support of the course as those that were used to support the denial of Cuba's requests. Recognition of Cuban independence, or intervention in favor of the Cubans, would have been the equivalent of the grant of belligerent rights. But the policy adopted, and the course pursued, did not serve to avert war with Spain. The story of that war has been written by many, and is not for inclusion here. The treaty of peace was signed, in Paris, on December 10, 1898, duly ratified by both parties in the following months, and was finally proclaimed on April 11, 1899. The war was over, but its definite termination was officially declared on the anniversary of the issuance of President McKinley's war message. On January 1, 1899, the American flag was hoisted throughout the island, as a signal of full authority, but subject to the provisions of the Teller Amendment to the Joint Resolution of Congress, of April 20, 1898, thus:

"That the United States hereby disclaims any disposition or intention to exercise sovereignty, jurisdiction, or control over said Island except for the pacification thereof, and asserts its determination, when that is accomplished, to leave the government and control of the Island to its people."

At twelve o'clock, noon, on the 20th of May, 1902, there was gathered in the State Apartment of the Palace occupied by many Spanish Governors-General, the officials of the United States, the elected officials of the new Cuban Republic, and a limited number of guests. In that same apartment, General Castellanos signed the abdication of Spanish authority. In its turn, pursuant to its pledges, the United States transferred authority to the President of the Cuban Republic. Four centuries of subjection, and a century of protest and struggle, were there and then ended, and Cuba joined the sisterhood of independent nations.

XI

FILIBUSTERING

The term "filibuster" affords an interesting example of the way in which words and their uses become twisted into something altogether different from their original meaning. It comes from a Dutch word, several centuries old, *vrijbuiter*, or free vessel or boat. It got somehow into English as "freebooter," and into Spanish as *filibustero*. The original referred to piracy. Two or three centuries later, it meant an engagement in unauthorized and illegal warfare against foreign States, in effect, piratical invasions. In time, it came into use to describe the supply of military material to revolutionists, and finally to obstruction in legislative proceedings. In his message of June 13, 1870, President Grant said that "the duty of opposition to filibustering has been admitted by every President. Washington encountered the efforts of Genet and the French revolutionists; John Adams, the projects of Miranda; Jefferson, the schemes of Aaron Burr. Madison and subsequent Presidents had to deal with the question of foreign enlistment and equipment in the United States, and since the days of John Quincy Adams it has been one of the constant cares of the Government in the United States to prevent piratical expeditions against the feeble Spanish American Republics from leaving our shores."

In 1806, Francisco Miranda, a Venezuelan patriot whose revolutionary activities preceded those of Simon Bolivar, sailed from New York on what would have been called, some years later, a filibustering expedition. His three vessels were manned chiefly by Americans. There are always those whose love of excitement and adventure, sometimes mixed with an active sympathy for an under dog, leads them to engage in such an enterprise. This one was productive of no important results. There were plenty of American pirates and privateers in earlier days, but I have found no record of any earlier actual expedition whose purpose was the creation of a new republic. But during the next hundred years, including the considerable number of Americans who have engaged in the present disorder in Mexico, such enterprises have been numerous. Among the most notable are the several Lopez expeditions to Cuba, about 1850, and the Walker expeditions to Lower California, Nicaragua, and Honduras, a few years later. The steamer *Virginius*, to which reference is made in another chapter, was engaged in filibustering when she was captured, in 1873, and many of her crew and passengers unlawfully executed, by Spanish authority, in Santiago. But that was only one of many similar enterprises during the Ten Years' War in Cuba. It is very doubtful if the war could have continued as it did without them. During our own Civil War, we called such industries "blockade-running," but it was all quite the same sort of thing. The Confederate army needed arms, ammunition, medicine, and supplies of many kinds. On April 19, 1861, President Lincoln proclaimed a blockade of the ports of the seceded States, with a supplementary proclamation on the 27th that completed the line, and thus tied the South hand and foot. In his *History of the United States*, Elson notes that raw cotton could be bought in Southern ports for four cents a pound while it was worth $2.50 a pound in Liverpool, and that a ton of salt worth seven or eight dollars in Nassau, a few miles off the coast, was worth $1700 in gold in Richmond before the close of the war, all because of the blockade.

There is, naturally, a lack of detail regarding the many expeditions, large and small, of the Ten Years' War, but they began soon after the opening of hostilities. In his *Diary*, Gideon Welles notes, under date of April 7, 1869, the prevalence of "rumors of illegal expeditions fitting out in our country to aid the Cuban insurgents," and states that "our countrymen are in sympathy with them." In December, of that year, President Grant reported that a number of illegal expeditions had been broken up, but did not refer to those that had succeeded. In October, 1870, he issued a general proclamation, without specific reference to Cuba, warning all persons against engagement in such expeditions. During the years of the war, Spanish warships, at different times, seized American vessels, a proceeding which led to some active diplomatic negotiation, and which, on several occasions, threatened to involve this country in war with Spain. The problem of the industry variously known as filibustering, blockade-running, gun-running, and the shipment of contraband, has two ends. There is, first, the task of getting the shipment out of one country, and, second, the task of getting it into another country. While it is generally classed as an unlawful enterprise, there frequently arises a difficulty in proving violation of law, even when goods are seized and the participants arrested. There is, perhaps, a moral question involved also. Such shipments may be a violation of the law. They are generally so regarded. But they may be, as in the case of the struggling Cubans, struggling against actual and generally admitted wrongs, the only means of serving a worthy and commendable end. There is no doubt that, in Cuba's revolution of 1895, Americans who knew about the work were prone to regard a successful expedition to the island with satisfaction if not with glee. They were inclined to regard those engaged as worthy patriots rather than as law-breakers.

Under date of February 23, 1898, the House of Representatives requested the Secretary of the Treasury to inform that body "at the earliest date practicable, if not incompatible with the public service, what has been done by the United States to prevent the conveyance to the Cubans of articles produced in the United States, and what to prevent 'filibustering,' and with what results, giving particulars, and at what expense to the United States." A reply was sent on the 28th. It makes a very good showing for the activities of the officials responsible for the prevention of such expeditions, but from all I can learn about the matter, it is quite incomplete. There were a number of excursions not set down in the official records. Sailing dates and time and place of arrival were not advertised in the daily papers.

The official statement shows that sixty reports of alleged filibustering expeditions were brought to the attention of the Treasury Department; that twenty-eight of them were frustrated through efforts of the Department; that five were frustrated by the United States Navy; four by Spain; two wrecked; one driven back by storm; one failed through a combination of causes; and seventeen that may be regarded as successful expeditions. The records of the Cuban *junta* very materially increase the number in the latter class. The despatch of these expeditions was a three-cornered battle of wits. The groups engaged were the officials of the United States, the representatives of Spain, and the agents of the revolution. The United States employed the revenue service and the navy, aided on land by the Customs Service, the Secret Service, and other Federal officers. The official representatives of Spain employed scores of detectives and Spanish spies. The Cuban group sought to outwit them all, and succeeded remarkably well in doing so. A part of the story has been told, with general correctness, in a little volume entitled *A Captain Unafraid*, described as *The Strange Adventures of Dynamite Johnny O'Brien*. This man, really a remarkable man in his special line, was born in New York, in 1837, and, at the time this is written, is still living. He was born and grew to boyhood in the shadow of the numerous shipyards then in active operation along the East River. The yards were his playground. At thirteen years of age, he ran away and went to see as cook on a fishing sloop. He admits that he could not then "cook a pot of water without burning it," but claims that he could catch cod-fish where no one else could find them. From fisherman, sailing-master on private yachts, schooner captain, and officer in the United States Navy in the Civil War, he became a licensed East River pilot in New York. He became what might be called a professional filibuster at the time of the revolution in Colombia, in 1885, following that with similar experience in a revolt in Honduras two years later. The Cubans landed a few expeditions in 1895, but a greater number were blocked. In March, 1896, they applied to O'Brien and engaged him to command the *Bermuda*, then lying in New York and ready to sail. Captain O'Brien reports that her cargo included "2,500 rifles, a 12-pounder Hotchkiss field-gun, 1,500 revolvers, 200 short carbines, 1000 pounds of dynamite, 1,200 *machetes*, and an abundance of ammunition." All was packed in boxes marked "codfish," and "medicines."

The *Bermuda* sailed the next morning, March 15, with O'Brien in command, cleared for Vera Cruz. The Cubans, including General Calixto Garcia, who were to go on the expedition, were sent to Atlantic City, there to engage a fishing sloop to take them off-shore where they would be picked up by the *Bermuda* on her way. The ship was under suspicion, and was followed down the bay by tugboats carrying United States marshals, customs officers, and newspaper reporters. O'Brien says: "They hung on to us down through the lower bay and out past Sandy Hook, without getting enough to pay for a pound of the coal they were furiously burning to keep up with us. I don't know how far they might have followed us, but when we were well clear of the Hook, a kind fortune sent along a blinding snow-storm, which soon chased them back home." General Garcia and his companions were picked up as planned, and that part of the enterprise was completed. The vessel was on its way. A somewhat roundabout route was taken in order to avoid any possible overhauling by naval or revenue ships. The point selected for the landing was a little harbor on the north coast about thirty miles from the eastern end of the island. The party included two

Cuban pilots, supposed to know the coast where they were to land. One of them proved to be a traitor and the other, O'Brien says, "was at best an ignoramus." The traitor, who, after the landing, paid for his offence with his life, tried to take them into the harbor of Baracoa, where lay five Spanish warships. But O'Brien knew the difference, as shown by his official charts, between the Cape Maisi light, visible for eighteen miles, and the Baracoa light, visible for only eight miles, and kicked the pilot off the bridge. The landing was begun at half-past ten at night, and completed about three o'clock in the morning, with five Spanish warships barely more than five miles away. The United States Treasury Department reported this expedition as "successful." The vessel then proceeded to Honduras, where it took on a cargo of bananas, and returned, under orders, to Philadelphia, the home city of its owner, Mr. John D. Hart. Arrests were made soon after the arrival, including Hart, the owner of the vessel, O'Brien, and his mate, and General Emilio Nuñez who accompanied the expedition as the representative of the *junta*. The case was transferred from the courts in Philadelphia to New York, and there duly heard. The alleged offenders were defended by Horatio Rubens, Esq., of New York, the official counsel of the *junta*. One of the grounds of the defence was that the defendants might be guilty of smuggling arms into Cuba, but with that offence the courts of the United States had nothing to do. The jury disagreed. The indictments were held over the heads of the members of the group, but no further action was taken, and two or three years later the case was dismissed by order of the Attorney General of the United States.

This expedition fairly illustrates the science of filibustering in its elementary form, a clearance with some attendant risk; a voyage with possibility of interference at any time; and a landing made with still greater risk and danger of capture. The trip had been made so successfully and with such full satisfaction to the promoters that the *junta* urged O'Brien to remain with them as long as there should be need for his services, and he agreed to do so. A department of expeditions was organized under the general control of Emilio Nuñez, with O'Brien as navigator. Credit for the numerous successful expeditions that followed lies in differing degrees with Nuñez, Palma, Rubens, O'Brien, Hart, Cartaya, and others less well known in connection with the enterprises. But for the work they did, the risks they ran, Cuba's revolution must have failed. All of them risked jail sentences, and some of them risked their lives in ways perhaps even more dangerous than fighting in the field. The success of the *Bermuda* expedition, carried out by what may be called direct evasion, quite seriously disturbed the authorities in this country, and excited them to greater precautions and wider activity. Whatever may have been their personal feelings in the matter, it was their duty to see that the laws of the country were enforced as far as they could be. The players of the game for the Cubans met the new activities with complicated moves, many of which puzzled the watching officials, and landed a number of expeditions. Meanwhile, minor expeditions continued. The official report notes that on March 12, 1896, the *Commodore*, a 100-ton steamer, sailed from Charleston with men, arms, and ammunition, and landed them in Cuba.

The *Laurada*, a 900-ton steamer, was reported by the Spanish Legation as having sailed on May 9, meeting three tugs and two lighters, off the coast, from which were transferred men and arms. The report states that "some of the men landed in Cuba, but the larger part of the arms and ammunition was thrown into the sea," which may or may not have been the case. On May 23, the tug *Three Friends* left Jacksonville, took on men and arms from two small vessels waiting outside, and landed all in Cuba. A month later, and again two months later, the *Three Friends* repeated the trip from Florida ports. On June 17, the *Commodore* made another successful trip from Charleston.

While these and other minor expeditions were going on, the department of expeditions in New York was busy with a more extensive enterprise. An order was placed for 3000 rifles, 3,000,000 rounds of ammunition, 3 12-pound Hotchkiss field-guns and 600 shells, *machetes*, and several tons of dynamite. The steamer *Laurada* was chartered, and the ocean-going tug *Dauntless* was bought in Brunswick, Georgia. A part of the purchased munitions was ordered to New York, and the remainder, two car loads, shipped to Jacksonville by express. Ostensibly, the *Laurada* was to sail from Philadelphia to Jamaica for a cargo of fruit, a business in which she had at times engaged. Her actual instructions were to proceed to the vicinity of Barnegat, about forty miles from New York, and there, at sea, await orders. The arms and ammunition came down from Bridgeport on the regular boat from that city, and were left on board until night. There was no particular secrecy about the shipment, and detectives followed it. But when, at dark, the big gates of the dock were closed and locked and all seemed over for the day, the watchers assumed that nothing would be done until the next day, and went away. But, immediately after their departure, a big lighter slipped quietly into the dock across the wharf from the Bridgeport boat, a swarm of men appeared and, behind the closed gates, in the semi-darkness of the wharf, rushed boxes from steamer to lighter. The work was finished at midnight; a tug slipped up and attached a hawser to the lighter; and the cargo was on its way to Cuba. Johnny O'Brien was on the tug. The *Laurada* was met off Barnegat, as arranged, and the cargo and about fifty Cubans put on board of her. She was ordered to proceed slowly to Navassa Island where the *Dauntless* would meet her. General Nuñez and O'Brien returned to New York on the tug, and while the detectives suspected that something had been done, they had no clue whatever to guide them. Nuñez and O'Brien started immediately for Charleston, with detectives at their heels. The *Commodore*, a tug then owned by the Cubans, lay in the harbor of that city, with a revenue cutter standing guard over her. She was ordered to get up steam and to go through all the motions of an immediate departure. But this was a ruse to draw attention away from the actual operations. Rubens, meanwhile, had gone to Jacksonville where he busied himself in convincing the authorities that the tug *Three Friends* was about to get away with an expedition. With one revenue cutter watching the *Commodore* in Charleston, the other cutter in the neighborhood was engaged in watching the *Three Friends* in Jacksonville, thus leaving a clear coast between those cities. In Charleston were about seventy-five Cubans waiting a chance to get to the island.

O'Brien states that about twenty-five detectives were following their party. Late in the afternoon of August 13, while the smoke was pouring from the funnels of the *Commodore*, the regular south-bound train pulled out of the city. Its rear car was a reserved coach carrying the Cuban party, numbering a hundred or so. Detectives tried to enter, but were told that it was a private car, which it was. They went along in the forward cars. At ten o'clock that night, the train reached Callahan, where the Coast Line crossed the Seaboard Air Line. While the train was halted for the crossing, that rear car was quietly uncoupled. The train went on, detectives and all. The railroad arrangements were effected through the invaluable assistance of Mr. Alphonso Fritot, a local railway man whose authority enabled him to do with trains and train movement whatever he saw fit. He was himself of Cuban birth, though of French-American parentage, with ample reason, both personal and patriotic, for serving his Cuban friends, and his services were beyond measure. By his orders, when that train with its band of detectives had pulled away for Jacksonville, an engine picked up the detached car and ran it over to the Coast Line. A few miles away, it collected from a blind siding the two cars of arms and ammunition shipped some days before, from Bridgeport. A little further on, the line crossed the Satilla River. There lay the *Dauntless*, purchased by Rubens. Steam was up, and a quick job was made of transferring cargo and men from train to boat. Another tug brought a supply of coal, and soon after sunrise another expedition was on its way to Cuba. All this may be very immoral, but some who were on the expedition have told me that it was at least tremendously exciting.

On August 17, the passengers and cargo were landed on the Cuban coast near Nuevitas. The tug then proceeded to Navassa Island to meet the *Laurada*. Half of the men and half of the cargo of the steamer were transferred to the tug, and all were safely landed in a little cove a few miles west of Santiago. The landing was made in broad daylight. There were a number of Spanish naval vessels in Santiago harbor, and the city itself was filled with Spanish troops. The tug then returned for the remainder of the *Laurada's* passengers and cargo, all of which were landed a few days later at the place of the earlier landing. The *Laurada* went on to Jamaica and loaded with bananas, with which she sailed for Charleston. Arrests were made as a result of the expedition, and the owner of the ship, Mr. John D. Hart, was convicted and sentenced to sixteen months in the penitentiary. After serving four months of his term, a pardon was secured. He is said to be the only one, out of all those engaged in the many expeditions, who was actually convicted, and his only offence was the chartering of his ships to the Cuban revolutionists. The *Dauntless* was seized on her return to Jacksonville, but was soon released. An effort was made to indict O'Brien, but there was too much sympathy for the Cubans in Florida, where the effort was made. A number of minor expeditions were carried out in the next few months, by the *Dauntless*, the *Three Friends*, and the *Commodore*, the latter being wrecked in the last week in December.

In February, 1897, another complicated manoeuvre was successfully executed. This involved the use of the *Bermuda*, the *Laurada*, and no less than seven smaller auxilliary vessels, tugs, lighters, and schooners. Rut the *Laurada* landed the cargo on the north-eastern coast of the island. As O'Brien tells the story, this successful expedition so angered Captain-General Weyler, then the ruler of the island, that he sent a message to the daring filibuster, through an American newspaper man, somewhat as follows: "Tell O'Brien that we will get him, sooner or later, and when we do, instead of having him shot along with his Cuban companions, I am going to have him ignominiously hanged from the flag-pole at Cabaña, in full view of the city." Cabaña is the old fortress across the bay, visible from nearly all parts of Havana. To this, O'Brien sent reply saying: "To show my contempt for you and all who take orders from you, I will make a landing within plain sight of Havana on my next trip to Cuba. I may even land an expedition inside of the harbor and take you away a prisoner. If we should capture you, which is much more likely than that you will ever capture me, I will have you chopped up into small pieces and fed to the fires of the *Dauntless*." A few months later, this little Irishman, whom Weyler denounced as a "bloodthirsty, dare-devil," and who may have been a dare-devil but was not bloodthirsty, actually carried out a part of this seemingly reckless threat. He landed a cargo within a mile and a half of Morro Castle.

By this time, vessels of the United States navy were employed, supplementing the work of the Revenue Service. This, of course, added both difficulty and danger to the work. In March and April, several expeditions were interrupted. For the Spanish blockade of the Cuban coast, there was only contempt. Captain O'Brien told a naval officer that if the navy and the revenue cutters would let him alone he would "advertise the time and place of departure, carry excursions on every trip, and guarantee that every expedition would be landed on time." In May, 1897, two carloads of arms and ammunition were shipped from New York to Jacksonville, but, by the authority of Mr. Fritot, they were quietly dropped from the train at a junction point, and sent to Wilmington, N.C. Their contents were transferred to the tug *Alexander Jones*, and that boat proceeded nonchalantly down the river. Soon afterward, an old schooner, the *John D. Long*, loaded with coal, followed the tug. Two revenue cutters were on hand, but there was nothing in the movements of these vessels to excite their interest. Off shore, the tug attached a towline to the schooner that was carrying its coal supply, its own bunkers being crammed with guns and cartridges. Off Palm Beach, General Nuñez and some sixty Cubans were taken from a fishing boat, according to a prearranged plan. Two days later, at an agreed upon place, they were joined by the *Dauntless* which had slipped out of Jacksonville. The excursion was then complete. About half the cargo of the *Jones* was transferred to the *Dauntless* and was landed, May 21, a few miles east of Nuevitas. A second trip took the remainder of the cargo of the *Jones* and most of the Cuban passengers, and landed the lot under the very guns, such as they were, of Morro Castle, and within about three miles of the Palace of Captain-General Weyler. All that time, a force of insurgents under Rodriguez and Aurenguren was operating in that immediate vicinity, and was in great need of the supplies thus obtained. Some of the dynamite then landed was used the next day to blow up a train on which Weyler was supposed to be travelling, but in their haste the Cubans got one train ahead of that carrying the official party. The row that Weyler made about this landing will probably never be forgotten by the subordinates who were the immediate victims of his rage.

These are only a few of the many expeditions, successful and unsuccessful, made during those three eventful years. The Treasury Department report of February 28, 1898, gives seventeen successful operations. As a matter of fact, more than forty landings were made, although in a few cases a single expedition accounted for two, and in one or two instances for three landings. The experiences run through the entire gamut of human emotions, from absurdity to tragedy. The former is illustrated by the case of the *Dauntless* when she was held up by a vessel of the United States navy, and boarded by one of the officers of the ship. He examined the tug from stem to stern, sat on boxes of ammunition which seemed to him to be boxes of sardines, stumbled over packages of rifles from which butts and muzzles protruded; and failed utterly to find anything that could be regarded as contraband. The mere fact that a vessel is engaged in transporting arms and ammunition does not, of necessity, bring it within reach of the law. But that particular vessel was a good deal more than under suspicion; it was under the closest surveillance and open to the sharpest scrutiny. The temporary myopia of that particular lieutenant of the United States navy was no more than an outward and visible sign of a well-developed sense of humor, and an indication of at least a personal sympathy for the Cubans in their struggle. Tragedy is illustrated by the disaster to the steamer *Tillie*. One day, late in January, 1898, this vessel, lying off the end of Long Island, took on one of the largest cargoes ever started on a filibustering expedition to Cuba. The cause is not known, but soon after starting a leak developed, beyond the capacity of the pumps. A heavy sea was running, and disaster was soon inevitable. The cargo was thrown overboard to lighten the ship and the vessel was headed for the shore on the chance that it might float until it could be beached. The water in the ship increased rapidly, and extinguished the fires under the boilers; the wind, blowing a high gale, swung into the northwest, thus driving the now helpless hulk out to sea. Huge combing waves swept the decks from end to end. O'Brien tells the story: "We looked in vain for another craft of any kind, and by the middle of the afternoon it seemed as though it was all up with us, for there was not much daylight left, and with her deck almost awash it was impossible that the *Tillie* should keep afloat all night. The gale had swept us rapidly out to sea. The wind, which was filled with icy needles, had kicked up a wild cross-sea, and it was more comfortable to go down with the ship than even to think of trying to escape in the boats." At last, when there seemed no longer any hope of rescue, the big five-masted schooner *Governor Ames* came plunging through the heaving seas, and, by masterly seamanship and good fortune, backed by the heroism of her commander and crew, succeeded in taking off all except four, who went down with the ship. But the work went on. There is not space here to tell of the several vessels whose names, through the engagement of the craft in these enterprises, became as familiar to newspaper readers as are the names of ocean liners today. A few months later, the United States Government sent its ships and its men to help those who, for three hard years, had struggled for national independence.

XII

THE STORY OF SUGAR

Chemically, sugar is a compound belonging to the group of carbohydrates, or organic compounds of carbon with oxygen and hydrogen. The group includes sugars, starches, gums, and celluloses. Sugar is a product of the vegetable kingdom, of plants, trees, root crops, etc. It is found in and is producible from many growths. As a laboratory process, it is obtainable from many sources, but, commercially, it is derived from only two, the sugar cane and the beet root. This statement, however, has a certain limitation in that it omits such products as maple sugar, malt sugar, milk sugar, and others having commercial or chemical uses on a limited scale. But it is only with the crystallized sucrose, the familiar sugar of the market and the household, that we are dealing here. The output of the other sugars is measurable in hundreds or even thousands of pounds, but the output of the sugar of commerce is measured in millions of tons. Long experience proves that the desired substance is most readily, most abundantly, and most cheaply, obtained from the juices of the plant commonly known as sugar cane, and from the vegetable known as the sugar beet.

The mechanical processes employed in producing sugar from cane and from beets, are practically the same. They are, broadly, the extraction or expression of the juices, their clarification and evaporation, and crystallization. These processes produce what is called "raw sugar," of varying percentages of sucrose content. Following them, there comes, for American uses, the process of refining, of removing the so-called impurities and foreign substances, and the final production of sugar in the shape of white crystals of different size, of sugar as powdered, cube, loaf, or other form. In the case of cane sugar, this is usually a secondary operation not conducted in the original mill. In the case of beet sugar, production is not infrequently a continuous operation in the same mill, from the beet root to the bagged or barrelled sugar ready for the market. The final product from both cane and beet is practically the same. Pure sugar is pure sugar, whatever its source. In the commercial production, on large scale, there remains a small fraction of molasses or other harmless substances, indistinguishable by sight, taste, or smell. With that fraction removed and an absolute 100 per cent. secured, there would be no way by which the particular origin could be determined. For all practical purposes, the sugar of commerce, whether from cane or beet, is pure sugar. It is doubtful if an adulterated sugar can be found in the United States, notwithstanding the tales of the grocer who "sands" his sugar, and of the producer who adds *terra alba* or some other adulterant. In some countries of Europe and elsewhere, there are sugars of inferior grades, of 85 or 90 or more degrees of sugar purity, but they are known as such and are sold at prices adjusted to their quality. Sugars of that class are obtainable in this country, but they are wanted almost exclusively for particular industrial purposes, for their glucose rather than their sucrose content. The

American household, whether the home of the rich or of the poor, demands the well-known white sugar of established purity.

There is still obtainable, in this country, but in limited quantity, a sugar very pleasantly remembered by many who have reached or passed middle age. It was variously known as "Muscovado" sugar, or as "plantation sugar," sometimes as "coffee" or "coffee crushed." It was a sugar somewhat sweeter to the taste than the white sugar, by reason of the presence of a percentage of molasses. It was a superior sugar for certain kitchen products, for pies, certain kinds of cake, etc. It has many times been urged in Congress that the employment of what is known as the Dutch Standard, now abolished, excluded this sugar from our market. This is not at all the fact. The disappearance of the commodity is due solely to change in the mechanical methods of sugar production. It would be quite impossible to supply the world's sugar demand by the old "open kettle" process by which that sugar was made. The quality of sugar is easily tested by any one who has a spoonful of sugar and a glass of water. If the sugar dissolves entirely, and dissolves without discoloring the water, it may be accepted as a pure sugar.

In his book on *The World's Cane Sugar Industry—Past and Present*, Mr. H.C. Prinsen Geerligs, a recognized expert authority on the subject, gives an elaborate history of the origin and development of the industry. His chapters on those branches are much too long for inclusion in full, but the following extracts tell the story in general outline. He states that the probability that sugar cane originally came from India is very strong, "as only the ancient literature of that country mentions sugar cane, while we know for certain that it was conveyed (from there) to other countries by travellers and sailors." The plant appears in Hindu mythology. A certain prince expressed a desire to be translated to heaven during his lifetime, but Indra, the monarch of the celestial regions, refused to admit him. A famous Hindu hermit, Vishva Mitra, prepared a temporary paradise for the prince, and for his use created the sugar cane as a heavenly food during his occupation of the place. The abode was afterward demolished, but the delectable plant, and a few other luxuries, were "spread all over the land of mortals as a permanent memorial of Vishva Mitra's miraculous deeds." In the time of Alexander the Great (356-323 B.C.) there appear tales of "a reed growing in India which produced honey without the aid of bees."

The early references are to sugar cane and not to cane sugar. While there may have been earlier experiences, the history of sugar, as such, seems to begin in the 7th century (A.D.). There is a story that the Chinese Emperor, Tai Tsung (627-650 A.D.) sent people to Behar, in India, to learn the art of sugar manufacture. The Arabs and the Egyptians soon learned how to purify sugar by re-crystallization, and to manufacture sweetmeats from the purified sugar. Marco Polo, who visited China during the last quarter of the 13th Century, refers to "a great many sugar factories in South China, where sugar could be freely bought at low prices." The Mohammedan records of that period also show the manufacture, in India, of crystallized sugar and candy. The area of production at that time covered, generally, the entire Mediterranean coast. The crusaders found extensive plantations in Tripoli, Mesopotamia, Palestine, Syria, and elsewhere. The plant is said to have been introduced in Spain as early as the year 755. Its cultivation is said to have been a flourishing industry there in the year 1150. Through China, it was early extended to Japan, Formosa, and the Philippines. The records of the 14th Century show the production and distribution of sugar as an important commercial enterprise in the Mediterranean region. The Portuguese discoveries of the 15th Century carried the plant to the Azores, the Cape Verde islands, and to possessions in the Gulf of Guinea. The Spaniards took it to the Western Hemisphere in the early years of the 16th Century. The Portuguese took it to Brazil at about the same time. While a Chinese traveller, visiting Java in 424, reports the cultivation of sugar cane, it was not until more than twelve hundred years later that the island, now an important source of sugar supply, began the production of sugar as a commercial enterprise. By the end of the 18th Century there was what might be called a sugar belt, girdling the globe and extending, roughly, from thirty-five degrees north of the equator to thirty-five degrees south of that line. It was then a product of many of the countries within those limits. The supply of that time was obtained entirely from cane.

The early years of the 19th Century brought a new experience in the sugar business. That was the production of sugar, in commercial quantities, from beets. From that time until now, the commodity has been a political shuttlecock, the object of government bounties and the subject of taxation. In 1747, Herr Marggraf, of the Academy of Sciences, in Berlin, discovered the existence of crystallizable sugar in the juice of the beet and other roots. No practical use was made of the discovery until 1801 when a factory was established near Breslau, in Silesia. The European beet-sugar industry, that has since attained enormous proportions, had its actual beginning in the early years of the 19th Century. It was a result of the Napoleonic wars of that period. When the wars were ended, and the blockades raised, the industry was continued in France by the aid of premiums, differentials, and practically prohibitory tariffs. The activities in other European countries under similar conditions of governmental aid, came a little later. The total world supply of sugar, including cane and beet, less than 1,500,000 tons, even as recently as 1850, seems small in comparison with the world's requirement of about twelve times that quantity at the present time. The output of beet sugar was then only about 200,000 tons, as compared with a present production of approximately 8,000,000 tons. But sugar was then a costly luxury while it is today a cheaply supplied household necessity. As recently as 1870, the wholesale price of granulated sugar in New York was thirteen and a half cents a pound, or about three times the present average.

Cane sugar is produced in large or small quantities in some fifty different countries and islands. In many, the output is only for domestic consumption, or in quantity too small to warrant inclusion in the list of sources of commercial supply. Sixteen countries are included in the list of beet-sugar producers. Of these, all are in Europe with the exception of the United States and Canada. Only two countries, the United States and Spain, produce sugar from both beet and cane. British India leads in the production of cane sugar, with Cuba a close second on the list, and Java the third. In their total, these three countries supply about two-thirds of the world's total output of cane sugar. Hawaii and Porto Rico, in that order, stand next on the list of producers. Under normal conditions, Germany leads in beet-sugar production, with Russia second, Austria-Hungary third, France fourth, and the United States fifth, with Belgium, the Netherlands, Italy, Sweden, and Denmark following. The island of Cuba is the most important source of commercial cane sugar. Immediately before the revolution of 1895, its output a little exceeded a million tons. The derangement caused by that experience covered several years, and it was not until 1903 that so large a crop was again made. Since that time, the output has more than doubled. The increase is attributable to the large increase in demand in the United States, and to the advantage given Cuban sugar in this market by the reciprocity treaty of 1903. Practically all of Cuba's export product is in the class commonly known as 96 degree centrifugals, that is, raw sugar of 96 per cent, or thereabout, of sugar content. Under normal conditions, nearly all of Cuba's shipments are to the United States. The sugar industry was introduced in Cuba very soon after the permanent settlement of the island, by Spaniards, in the early years of the 16th Century, but it was not until two hundred and fifty years later that Spain's restrictive and oppressive colonial policy made even its fair extension possible. In 1760, two and a half centuries after the first settlement, the sugar exports of the island were a little less than 4,400 tons. In 1790, they were a little more than 14,000 tons. Some relaxation of the laws regulating production and exportation, made possible an increase to 41,000 tons in 1802, and further relaxation made possible, in 1850, an output somewhat unreliably reported as 223,000 tons. It reached 632,000 tons in 1890, and the stimulus of the "free sugar" schedule of the United States brought it, in the next few years, to more than a million tons. Production in recent years has averaged about 2,500,000 tons.

In forty years, only a little more than a single generation, the world's supply of sugar has been multiplied by five, from a little more than three million tons a year to nearly eighteen million tons. The total world output in 1875 would not today supply the demand of the United States alone. This increase in production has been made possible by improvements in the methods and the machinery of manufacture. Until quite recently, primitive methods were employed, much like those used in the production of maple sugar on the farm, although on larger scale. More attention has been paid to varieties of the plant and some, though no very great, change has been made in field processes. In Cuba, the cane is planted in vast areas, in thousands of acres. Some of the estates plant and cultivate their own fields, and grind the cane in their own mills. Others, known as "*colonos*," are planters only, the crop being sold to the mills commonly called "*centrales*." In its general appearance, a field of sugar-cane looks quite like a field of corn, but the method of cultivation is somewhat different. The slow oxen are still commonly used for plowing and for carts. This is not because of any lack of progressive spirit, but because experience has shown that, under all conditions of the industry, the ox makes the most satisfactory and economical motive power, notwithstanding his lack of pace.

The Encyclopædia describes sugar-cane as "a member of the grass family, known botanically as *Saccharum officinarum*. It is a tall, perennial grass-like plant, giving off numerous erect stems 6 to 12 feet or more in height, from a thick solid jointed root-stalk." The ground is plowed in rows in which, not seed, but a stalk of cane is lightly buried. The rootlets and the new cane spring from the joints of the planted stalk which is laid flat and lengthwise of the row. It takes from a year to a year and a half for the stalk to mature sufficiently for cutting and grinding. Several cuttings, and sometimes many, are made from a single planting. There are tales of fields on which cane has grown for forty years without re-planting. A few years ago, ten or fifteen years was not an unusual period. The present tendency is toward more frequent planting, but not annual, as offering a better chance for stronger cane with a larger sugar content. The whole process of cultivation and field treatment is hard, heavy work, most of it very hard work. Probably the hardest and heaviest is the cutting. This is done with a long, heavy-bladed knife, the *machete*. The stalk, from an inch to two inches in thickness, is chopped down near the root, the heavy knife swung with cut after cut, under a burning sun. Only the strongest can stand it, a wearying, back-breaking task. After cutting, the stalk is trimmed and loaded on carts to be hauled, according to distance, either directly to the mill or to the railway running thereto. The large estates have their own railway systems running to all the fields of the plantation. These are private lines operated only for economy in cane transportation. Most of the crushing mills measure their daily consumption of cane in thousands of tons. While every precaution is taken, there are occasional fires. In planting, wide "fire lanes," or uncultivated strips are left to prevent the spread of fire if it occurs.

Mill installations vary on the different plantations, but the general principle of operation is the same on all. The first process is the extraction of the juice that carries the sugar. It is probable that this was originally done in hand mortars. Next came the passing of the cane between wooden rollers turned by ox power, the rollers standing upright and connected with a projecting shaft or beam to the outer end of which the animal was attached, to plod around and around while the cane was fed between the rollers. The present system is merely an expansion of that old principle. At the mill, the stalks are dumped, by carload or by cartload, into a channel through which they are mechanically conveyed to huge rollers, placed horizontally, arranged in pairs or in sets of three, and slowly turned by powerful engines. The larger mills have a series of these rollers, two, three, or even four sets, the stalks passing from one to another for the expression of every possible drop of the juice, up to the point where the cost of juice extraction exceeds the value of the juice obtained. The expressed juices are collected in troughs through which they are run to the next operation. The crushed stalks, then known as *bagasse*, are conveyed to the huge boilers where they are used as fuel for the generation of the steam required in the various operations, from the feeding and the turning of the rollers, to the device from which the final product, the crystallized sugar, is poured into bags ready for shipment. All this is a seasonal enterprise. The cane grows throughout the year, but it begins to ripen in December. Then the mills start up and run until the rains of the next May or June suspend further operations. It then becomes impossible to haul the cane over the heavily mired roads from the muddy fields. Usually, only a few mills begin their work in December, and early June usually sees most of them shut down. The beginning of the rainy season is not uniform, and there are mills in eastern Cuba that sometimes run into July and even into August. But the general grinding season may be given as of about five months duration, and busy months they are. The work goes on night and day.

The next step is the treatment of the juices expressed by the rollers and collected in the troughs that carry it onward. The operations are highly technical, and different methods are employed in different mills. The first operation is one of purification. The juice, as it comes from the rollers, carries such materials as glucose, salts, organic acids, and other impurities, that must be removed. For this, lime is the principal agent. The details of it all would be as tedious here as they are complicated in the mill. The percentages of the different impurities vary with the variation of the soils in which the cane is grown. The next step, following clarification, is evaporation, the boiling out of a large percentage of the water carried in the juice. For this purpose, a vacuum system is used, making possible a more rapid evaporation with a smaller expenditure of fuel. These two operations, clarification and evaporation by the use of the vacuum, are merely improved methods for doing, on a large scale, what was formerly done by boiling in pans or kettles, on a small scale. That method is still used in many parts of the world, and even in the United States, in a small way. For special reasons, it is still used on some of the Louisiana plantations; it is common in the farm production of sorghum molasses in the South; and in the manufacture of maple sugar in the North. In those places, the juices are boiled in open pans or kettles, the impurities skimmed off as they rise, and the boiling, for evaporation, is continued until a proper consistency is reached, for molasses in the case of sorghum and for crystallization in the case of plantation and maple sugars. There is an old story of an erratic New England trader, in Newburyport, who called himself Lord Timothy Dexter. In one of his shipments to the West Indies, a hundred and fifty years ago, this picturesque individual included a consignment of "warming pans," shallow metal basins with a cover and a long wooden handle, used for warming beds on cold winter nights. The basin was filled with coals from the fireplace, and then moved about between the sheets to take off the chill. He was not a little ridiculed by his acquaintances for sending such merchandise where it could not possibly be needed, but it is said that he made considerable money out of his enterprise. With the covers removed, the long-handled, shallow basins proved admirably adapted for use in skimming the sugar in the boiling-pans. But the old-fashioned method would be impossible today.

The different operations are too complicated and too technical for more than a reference to the purpose of the successive processes. Clarification and evaporation having been completed, the next step is crystallization, also a complicated operation. When this is done, there remains a dark brown mass consisting of sugar crystals and molasses, and the next step is the removal of all except a small percentage of the molasses. This is accomplished by what are called the centrifugals, deep bowls with perforated walls, whirled at two or three thousand revolutions a minute. This expels the greater part of the molasses, and leaves a mass of yellow-brown crystals, the coloring being due to the molasses remaining. This is the raw sugar of commerce. Most of Cuba's raw product is classed as "96 degree centrifugals," that is, the raw sugar, as it comes from the centrifugal machines and is bagged for shipment, is of 96 degrees of sugar purity. This is shipped to market, usually in full cargo lots. There it goes to the refineries, where it is melted, clarified, evaporated, and crystallized. This second clarification removes practically everything except the pure crystallized sugar of the market and the table. It is then an article of daily use in every household, and a subject of everlasting debate in Congress.

XIII

VARIOUS PRODUCTS AND INDUSTRIES

The Encyclopædia Britannica states that "although the fact has been controverted, there cannot be a doubt that the knowledge of tobacco and its uses came to the rest of the world from America. As the continent was opened up and explored, it became evident that the consumption of tobacco, especially by smoking, was a universal and immemorial usage, in many cases bound up with the most significant and solemn tribal ceremonials." The name "tobacco" was originally the name of the appliance in which it was smoked and not of the plant itself, just as the term "chowder" comes from the vessel (*chaudière*) in which the compound was prepared. The tobacco plant was first taken to Europe in 1558, by Francisco Fernandez, a physician who had been sent to Mexico by Philip II to investigate the products of that country. The English, however, appear to have been the first Europeans to adopt the smoking habit, and Sir Walter Raleigh was notable for his indulgence in the weed. He is said to have called for a solacing pipe just before his execution. Very soon after their arrival, in 1607, the Virginia settlers engaged in the cultivation of tobacco, and it soon became the most important commercial product of the colony. Smoking, as practiced in this country, appears to have been largely, and perhaps only, by means of pipes generally similar to those now in use. The contents of ancient Indian mounds, or tumuli, opened in Ohio, Indiana, Illinois, and Iowa, show the use of pipes by the aborigines probably centuries before the discoveries by Columbus. Many were elaborately carved in porphyry or some other hard stone, while others were made of baked clay. Others, many of them also elaborately carved and ornamented, have been found in Mexico. Roman antiquities show many pipes, but they do not show the use of tobacco. It is assumed that they were used for burning incense, or for smoking some aromatic herb or hemp.

The first knowledge of the use of the plant in Cuba was in November, 1492, when Columbus, on landing near Nuevitas, sent his messengers inland to greet the supposed ruler of a supposed great Asiatic empire. Washington Irving thus reports the story as it was told by Navarete, the Spanish historian. Referring to those messengers, he says: "They beheld several of the natives going about with firebrands in their hands, and certain dried herbs which they rolled up in a leaf, and lighting one end, put the other in their mouths, and continued exhaling and puffing out the smoke. A roll of this kind they called a tobacco, a name since transferred to the plant of which the rolls were made. The Spaniards, although prepared to meet with wonders, were struck with astonishment at this singular and apparently nauseous indulgence." A few years later, a different method was reported, by Columbus, as employed in Hispaniola. This consisted of inhaling the fumes of the leaf through a Y-shaped device applied to the nostrils. This operation is said to have produced intoxication and stupefaction, which appears to have been the desired result. The old name still continues in Cuba, and if a smoker wants a cigar, he will get it by calling for a "tobacco." The production of the plant is, next to sugar, Cuba's most important commercial industry. Its early history is only imperfectly known. There was probably very little commercial production during the 16th Century, for the reason that there was then no demand for it. The demand came in the first half of the 17th Century, and by the middle of that period tobacco was known and used in practically all civilized countries. The demand for it spread very rapidly, in spite of papal fulminations and penal enactments. For a time, in Russia, the noses of smokers were cut off. The early part of the 18th Century saw Cuba actively engaged in production and shipment. In 1717, Cuba's tobacco was made a monopoly of the Spanish Government. Under that system, production was regulated and prices were fixed by the agents of the government, in utter disregard of the welfare of the producers. As a result, several serious riots occurred. In 1723, a large number of planters refused to accept the terms offered by the officials, and destroyed the crops of those who did accept, a condition repeated in the State of Kentucky a few years ago, the only difference being that in the Cuban experience the monopolist was the Government, and in Kentucky it was a corporation. A few years later, in 1734, the Cuban monopoly was sold to Don José Tallapiedra who contracted to ship to Spain, annually, three million pounds of tobacco. The contract was afterward given to another, but control was resumed by the Crown, in 1760. Finally, in 1817, cultivation and trade were declared to be free, subject only to taxation.

In time, it became known that the choicest tobacco in the market came from the western end of Cuba, from the Province of Pinar del Rio. It was given a distinct name, *Vuelta Abajo*, a term variously translated but referring to the downward bend of the section of the island in which that grade is produced. Here is grown a tobacco that, thus far, has been impossible of production elsewhere. Many experiments have been tried, in Cuba and in other countries. Soils have been analyzed by chemists; seeds from the *Vuelta Abajo* have been planted; and localities have been sought where climatic conditions corresponded. No success has been attained. Nor is the crop of that region produced on an extensive scale, that is, the choicer leaf. Not all of the tobacco is of the finest grade, although most of it is of high quality. There are what may be called "patches" of ground, known to the experts, on which the best is produced, for reasons not yet clearly determined. The fact is well known, but the causes are somewhat mysterious. Nor does the plant of this region appear to be susceptible of improvement through any modern, scientific systems of cultivation. The quality deteriorates rather than improves as a result of artificial fertilizers. The people of the region, cultivating this special product through generation after generation, seem to have developed a peculiar instinct for its treatment. It is not impossible that a time may come when scientific soil selection, seed selection, special cultivation, irrigation, and other systems, singly or in combination, will make possible the production of a standardized high-grade leaf in much greater quantity than heretofore, but it seems little probable that anything so produced will excel or even equal the best produced by these expert *vegueros* by their indefinable but thorough knowledge of the minutest peculiarities of this peculiar plant. Thus far, it has not even been possible to produce it elsewhere in the island. It has been tried outside of the fairly defined area of its production, tried by men who knew it thoroughly within that area, tried from the same seed, from soils that seem quite the same. But all failed. Science may some day definitely locate the reasons, just as it may find the reason for deterioration in the quality of Cuban tobacco eastward from that area. The tobacco of Havana Province is excellent, but inferior to that of Pinar del Rio. The growth of Santa Clara Province is of good quality, but inferior to that of Havana Province, while the tobacco of eastern Cuba is little short of an offence to a discriminating taste.

Tobacco is grown from seeds, planted in specially prepared seed beds. Seeding is begun in the early autumn. When the young plant has attained a proper height, about eight or ten inches, it is removed to, and planted in, the field of its final growth. This preliminary process demands skill, knowledge, and careful attention equal, perhaps, to the requirements of the later stages. Experiments have been made with mechanical appliances, but most of the work is still done by hand, particularly in the area producing the better qualities of leaf. From the time of transplanting, it is watched with the greatest care. A constant battle is waged with weeds and insect life, and water must be brought if the season is too dry. If rains are excessive, as they sometimes are, the crop may be partly or wholly destroyed, as it was in the autumn of 1914. The plant matures in January, after four months of constant watchfulness and labor, in cultivation, pruning, and protection from worms and insects. When the leaves are properly ripened, the stalks are cut in sections, two leaves to a section. These are hung on poles and taken to the drying sheds where they are suspended for three or more weeks. The time of this process, and its results, depend upon moisture, temperature, and treatment. All this is again an operation demanding expert knowledge and constant care. When properly cured, the leaves are packed in bales of about 110 pounds each, and are then ready for the market. Because of the varying conditions under which the leaf is produced, from year to year, it is somewhat difficult to determine with any accuracy the increase in the industry. Broadly, the output appears to have been practically doubled in the last twenty years, a growth attributed to the new economic conditions, to the extension of transportation facilities that have made possible the opening of new areas to cultivation, and to the investment of capital, largely American capital. The exports show, generally, a material increase in sales of leaf tobacco and some decline in sales of cigars. The principal market for the leaf, for about 85 per cent of it, is in the United States where it is made, with more or less honesty, into "all-Havana" cigars. This country, however, takes only about a third of Cuba's cigar output. The United Kingdom takes about as much of that product as we do, and Germany, in normal times, takes about half as much. The remainder is widely scattered, and genuine imported Havana cigars are obtainable in all countries throughout the world. The total value of Cuba's yearly tobacco crop is from $40,000,000 to $50,000,000, including domestic consumption and foreign trade.

The story that all Cubans, men and women alike, are habitual and constant smokers, is not and never was true. Whatever it may have been in the past, I am inclined to think that smoking by women is more common in this country than it is in Cuba, particularly among the middle and upper social classes. I have seen many American and English women smoke in public, but never a Cuban woman. Nor is smoking by men without its exceptions. I doubt if the percentage of non-smokers in this country is any greater than it is in the island. There are many Cubans who do smoke, just as there are many Americans, Englishmen, Germans, and Russians. Those who watch on the street for a respectable Cuban woman with a cigar in her mouth, or even a cigarette, will be disappointed. Cuba's tobacco is known by the name of the region in which it is produced; the *Vuelta Abajo* of Pinar del Rio; the *Partidos* of Havana Province; the *Manicaragua* and the *Remedios* of Santa Clara; and the *Mayari* of Oriente. Until quite recently, when American organized capital secured control of many of the leading factories in Cuba, it was possible to identify a cigar, in size and shape, by some commonly employed name, such as *perfectos, conchas, panetelas, imperiales, londres,* etc. The old names still appear, but to them there has been added an almost interminable list in which the old distinction is almost lost. Lost, too, or submerged, are many of the old well-known names of manufacturers, names that were a guarantee of quality. There were also names for different qualities, almost invariably reliable, and for color that was supposed to mark the strength of the cigar. An accomplished smoker may still follow the old system and call for a cigar to his liking, by the use of the old terms and names made familiar by years of experience, but the general run of smokers can only select, from a hundred or more boxes bearing names and words that are unfamiliar or unknown, a cigar that he thinks looks like one that he wants. It may be a "*superba*" an "*imperial*" a "Wilson's Cabinet," or a "Havana Kid."

There is a wide difference in the dates given as the time of the introduction of the coffee plant in Cuba. One writer gives the year 1720, another gives 1748, and still another gives 1769. Others give various years near the end of the century. It was doubtless a minor industry for fifty years or more before that time, but it was given an impetus and began to assume commercial proportions during the closing years of the 18th Century. During that century, the industry was somewhat extensively carried on in the neighboring island of Santo Domingo. In 1790, a revolution broke out in that island, including Haiti, and lasted, with more or less violent activity, for nearly ten years. One result was the emigration to Cuba of a considerable number of refugees, many of them French. They settled in eastern Cuba, where conditions for coffee-growing are highly favorable. Knowing that industry from their experience with it in the adjacent island, these people naturally took it up in their new home. The cultivation of coffee in Cuba, prior to that time, was largely in the neighborhood of Havana, the region then of the greater settlement and development. For the next forty years or so, the industry developed and coffee assumed a considerable importance as an export commodity, in addition to the domestic supply. In 1840, there were more than two thousand coffee plantations, large and small, producing more than seventy million pounds of coffee, the greater part of which was exported. From about the middle of the century, the industry declined, in part because of lower prices due to increase in the world-supply through increased production in other countries, and in part, because of the larger chance of profit in the growing of sugar, an industry then showing an increased importance. Coffee culture has never been entirely suspended in the island, and efforts are made from time to time to revive it, but for many years Cuba has imported most of its coffee supply, the larger share being purchased from Porto Rico. It would be easily possible for Cuba to produce its entire requirement. There are few more beautiful sights in all the world than a field of coffee trees in blossom. One writer has likened it to "millions of snow drops scattered over a sea of green." They blossom, in Cuba, about the end of February or early in March, the fruit season and picking coming in the autumn. Coffee culture is an industry requiring great care and some knowledge, and the preparation of the berry for the market involves no less of care and knowledge. The quality of the Cuban berry is of the best. It is the misfortune of the people of the United States that very few of them really know anything about coffee and its qualities, notwithstanding the fact that they consume about a billion pounds a year, all except a small percentage of it being coffee of really inferior quality. But coffee, like cigars, pickles, or music, is largely a matter of individual preference.

Cuba produces a variety of vegetables, chiefly for domestic consumption, and many fruits, some of which are exported. There is also a limited production of grains. Among the tubers produced are sweet potatoes, white potatoes, yams, the arum and the yucca. From the latter is made starch and the cassava bread. The legumes are represented by varieties of beans and peas. The most extensively used food of the island people is rice, only a little of which is locally grown. The imports are valued at five or six million dollars yearly. Corn is grown in some quantity, but nearly two million dollars worth is imported yearly from the United States. There are fruits of many kinds. The banana is the most important of the group, and is grown throughout the island. It appears on the table of all, rich and poor, sometimes *au naturel* but more frequently cooked. There are many varieties, some of which are exported while others are practically unknown here. The Cuban mango is not of the best, but they are locally consumed by the million. Only a few of the best are produced and those command a fancy price even when they are obtainable. The aguacate, or alligator pear, is produced in abundance. Cocoanuts are a product largely of the eastern end of the island, although produced in fair supply elsewhere. The trees are victims of a disastrous bud disease that has attacked them in recent years causing heavy loss to growers.

Since the American occupation, considerable attention has been given, mainly by Americans, to the production of oranges, grape-fruit, and pineapples, in which a considerable industry has been developed. There are several varieties. The guava of Cuba makes a jelly that is superior to that produced from the fruit in any other land of my experience. If there is a better guava jelly produced anywhere, I should be pleased to sample it, more pleased to obtain a supply. But there is a difference in the product even there, just as there is a difference in currant or grape jelly produced here. It depends a good deal on the maker. Some of the best of my experience is made in the neighborhood of Santa Clara, but I have tried no Cuban *jalea de guayaba* that was not better than any I have had in the Far East or elsewhere. The *guanabana* is eaten in its natural state, but serves its best purpose as a flavor for ices or cooling drinks. There are a number of others, like the *anon*, the *zapote*, the *granadilla*, the *mamey*, etc., with which visitors may experiment or not as they see fit. Some like some of them and others like none of them. An excellent grade of cacao, the basis of chocolate and cocoa, is produced in somewhat limited quantity. The industry could easily be extended. In fact, there are many soil products not now grown in the island but which might be grown there, and many others now produced on small scale that could be produced in important quantities. That they are not now so produced is due to lack of both labor and capital. The industries of Cuba are, and always have been, specialized. Sugar, tobacco, and at a time coffee, have absorbed the capital and have afforded occupation for the greater number of the island people. The lack of transportation facilities in earlier years, and the system of land tenure, have made difficult if not impossible the establishment of any large number of independent small farmers. The day laborers in the tobacco fields and on sugar plantations have been unable to save enough money to buy a little farm and equip it even if the land could be purchased at all. Yet only a very small percentage of the area is actually under cultivation. Cuba now imports nearly $40,000,000 worth of alimentary substances, altogether too much for a country of its productive possibilities. It is true that a part of this, such as wheat flour for instance, cannot be produced on the island successfully, and that other commodities, such as rice, hog products, and some other articles, can be imported more cheaply than they can be produced locally. But the imports of foodstuffs are undoubtedly excessive, although there are good reasons for the present situation. It is a matter that will find adjustment in time.

The island has mineral resources of considerable value, although the number of products is limited. The Spanish discoverers did not find the precious metals for which they were seeking, and while gold has since been found, it has never appeared in quantity sufficient to warrant its exploitation. Silver discoveries have been reported, but not in quantity to pay for its extraction. Nothing is ever certain in those industries, but it is quite safe to assume that Cuba is not a land of precious metals. Copper was discovered in eastern Cuba as early as about the year 1530, and the mines near Santiago were operated as a Government monopoly for some two hundred years, when they were abandoned. They were idle for about a hundred years when, in 1830, an English company with a capital of $2,400,000 reopened them. It is officially reported that in the next forty years copper of a value of more than $50,000,000 was extracted and shipped. During that time, the mines were among the most notable in the world. In the meantime, ownership was transferred to a Spanish corporation organized in Havana. This concern became involved in litigation with the railway concerning freight charges, and this experience was followed by the Ten Years' War, in the early course of which the plant was destroyed and the mines flooded. In 1902, an American company was organized. It acquired practically all the copper property in the Cobre field and began operations on an extensive and expensive scale. A huge sum was spent in pumping thousands of tons of water from a depth of hundreds of feet, in new equipment for the mining operations, and in the construction of a smelter. The best that can be done is to hope that the investors will some day get their money back. Without any doubt, there is a large amount of copper there, and more in other parts of Oriente. So is there copper in Camaguey, Santa Clara, and Matanzas provinces. There are holes in the ground near the city of Camaguey that indicate profitable operations in earlier years. The metal is spread over a wide area in Pinar del Rio, and venturous spirits have spent many good Spanish pesos and still better American dollars in efforts to locate deposits big enough to pay for its excavation. Some of that class are at it even now, and one concern is reported as doing a profitable business.

The bitumens are represented in the island by asphalt, a low-grade coal, and seepages of petroleum. At least, several writers tell of coal in the vicinity of Havana, but the substance is probably only a particularly hard asphaltum. The only real coal property of which I have any knowledge is a quite recent discovery. The story was told me by the man whose money was sought to develop it. It was, by the way, an anthracite property. In response to an urgent invitation from a presumably reliable acquaintance, my friend took his car and journeyed westward into Pinar del Rio, through a charming country that he and I have many times enjoyed together. He picked up his coal-discovering friend in the city of Pinar del Rio, and proceeded into the country to inspect the coal-vein. At a number of points immediately alongside the highway, his companion alighted to scrape away a little of the surface of the earth and to return with a little lump of really high-grade anthracite. Such a substance had no proper business there, did not belong there geologically or otherwise. The explanation soon dawned upon my friend. They were following the line of an abandoned narrow-gauge railway, abandoned twenty years ago, along which had been dumped, at intervals, little piles of perfectly good anthracite, imported from Pennsylvania, for use by the portable engine used in the construction of the road. My friend declares that he is entirely ready at any time to swear that there are deposits of anthracite in Cuba. A very good quality of asphalt is obtained in different parts of the island, and considerable quantities have been shipped to the United States. Signs of petroleum deposits have been strong enough to induce investigation and expenditure. An American company is now at work drilling in Matanzas Province. The most extensive and promising mineral industry is iron, especially in eastern Cuba. Millions of tons of ore have been taken from the mountains along the shore between Santiago and Guantanamo, and the supply appears to be inexhaustible. The product is shipped to the United States, to a value of several millions of dollars yearly. A few years ago, other and apparently more extensive deposits were discovered in the northern section of Oriente, The field bought by the Pennsylvania Steel Company is estimated to contain 600,000,000 tons of ore. The Bethlehem Steel Company is the owner of another vast tract. The quality of these ores is excellent. In Oriente Province also are deposits of manganese of which considerable shipments have been made.

It is not possible in so brief a survey of Cuba's resources and industries to include all its present activities, to say nothing of its future possibilities. At the present time, the island is practically an extensive but only partly cultivated farm, producing mainly sugar and tobacco, with fruits and vegetables as a side line. The metal deposits supplement this, with promise of becoming increasingly valuable. The forest resources, commercially, are not great, although there are, and will continue to be, sales of mahogany and other fine hardwoods. Local manufacturing is on a comparatively limited scale. All cities and many towns have their artisans, the bakers, tailors, shoemakers, carpenters, and others. Cigar making is, of course, classed as a manufacturing enterprise, and so, for census purposes, is the conversion of the juice of the sugar-cane into sugar. A number of cities have breweries, ice factories, match factories, soap works, and other establishments large or small. All these, however, are incidental to the great industries of the soil, and the greater part of Cuba's requirements in the line of mill and factory products is imported. While little is done in the shipment of cattle or beef, Cuba is a natural cattle country. Water and nutritious grasses are abundant, and there are vast areas, now idle, that might well be utilized for stock-raising. There are, of course, just as there are elsewhere, various difficulties to be met, but they are met and overcome. There are insects and diseases, but these are controlled by properly applied scientific methods. There is open feeding throughout the entire year, so there is no need of barns or hay. The local cattle industry makes possible the shipment of some $2,500,000 worth of hides and skins annually. Other lines of industry worthy of mention, but not possible of detailed description here, include sponges, tortoise shell, honey, wax, molasses, and henequen or sisal. All these represent their individual thousands or hundreds of thousands of dollars, and their employment of scores or hundreds of wage-earners. Those who start for Cuba with a notion that the Cubans are an idle and lazy people, will do well to revise that notion. There is not the hustle that may be seen further north, but the results of Cuban activity, measured in dollars or in tons, fairly dispute the notion of any national indolence. When two and a half million people produce what is produced in Cuba, somebody has to work.

XIV

POLITICS, GOVERNMENT, AND COMMERCE

The British colonists in America were in large measure self-governing. This is notably true in their local affairs. The Spanish colonists were governed almost absolutely by the mother-country. A United States official publication reports that "all government control centred in the Council of the Indies and the King, and local self government, which was developed at an early stage in the English colonies, became practically impossible in the Spanish colonies, no matter to what extent it may have existed in theory. Special regulations, decrees, etc., modifying the application of the laws to the colonies or promulgating new laws were frequent, and their compilation in 1680 was published as Law of the Indies. This and the *Siete Partidas*, on which they were largely based, comprised the code under which the Spanish-American colonies were governed." There was a paper provision, during the greater part of the time, for a municipal electorate, the franchise being limited to a few of the largest tax-payers. In its practical operation, the system was nullified by the power vested in the appointed ruler. It was a highly effective centralized organization in which no man held office, high or low, who was not a mere instrument in the hands of the Governor-General. Under such an institution the Cubans had, of course, absolutely no experience in self-government. The rulers made laws and the people obeyed them; they imposed taxes and spent the money as they saw fit; many of them enriched themselves and their personally appointed official household throughout the island, at the expense of the tax-payers.

A competent observer has noted that such terms as "meeting," "mass-meeting," "self-government," and "home-rule," had no equivalent in the Spanish language. The first of these terms, distorted into "*mitin*," is now in common use, and its origin is obvious. Of theories, ideals, and intellectual conceptions, there was an abundance, but government based on beautiful dreams does not succeed in this practical world. Denied opportunity for free discussion of practical methods, the Cubans discussed theories in lyceums. Under the military government of the United States, from January 1, 1899, to May 20, 1902, there was freedom of speech and freedom of organization. The Cubans began to hold "*mitins*," but visions and beautiful theories characterized the addresses. Prior to the Ten Years' War (1868-1878), there were organizations more or less political in their nature, but the authorities were alert in preventing discussions of too practical a character. In 1865, a number of influential Cubans organized what has been somewhat inappropriately termed a "national party." It was not at all a party in our use of that term. Its purpose was to suggest and urge administrative and economic changes from the Cuban point of view. The suggestions were ignored and, a few years later, revolution was adopted as a means of emphasizing their importance. The result of the Ten Years' War was an assortment of pledges of greater political and economic freedom. Much was promised but little if anything was really granted. There was, however, a relaxation of the earlier absolutism, and under that there appeared a semblance of party organization, in the form of a Liberal party and a Union Constitutional party. There was no special difference in what might be called their platforms. Both focussed, in a somewhat general way, the political aspirations and the economic desires of the Cuban people, much the same aspirations and desires that had been manifested by complaint, protest, and occasional outbreak, for fifty years. National independence had no place in either. That came later, when an army in the field declared that if Spain would not grant independence, the island would be made so worthless a possession that Spain could not afford to hold it. A few years after their organization, the Liberals became the Cuban party, and so remained, and the Union Constitutionals became the Spanish party, the party of the immediate administration. Later on, the Liberal party became the Autonomist party, but Spain's concession of the demands of that group came too late, forced, not by the Autonomists but by the party of the Revolution that swept the island with fire and sword from Oriente to Pinar del Rio. The Autonomists sought what their name indicates; the Revolutionists demanded and secured national independence.

Shortly before the final dispersion of the Army of the Revolution, there was organized a body with the imposing title of *La Asamblea de Representantes del Ejercito Cubano*, or the Assembly of Representatives of the Cuban Army. It was composed of leaders of the different military divisions of that army, and included, as I recall it, thirty-one members. This group made no little trouble in the early days of the American occupation. It gathered in Havana, held meetings, declared itself the duly chosen and representative agent of the Cuban people, and demanded recognition as such by the American authorities. Some of its members even asserted that it constituted a *de facto* government, and held that the Americans should turn the whole affair over to them and promptly sail away. But their recognition was flatly refused by the authorities. At the time, I supported the authorities in this refusal, but afterward I felt less sure of the wisdom of the course. As a recognized body, it might have been useful; rejected, it made no little trouble. Transfer of control to its hands was quite out of the question, but recognition and co-operation might have proved helpful. That the body had a considerable representative quality, there is no doubt. Later, I found many of its members as members of the Constitutional Convention, and, still later, many of them have served in high official positions, as governors of provinces, members of Congress, in cabinet and in diplomatic positions. I am inclined to regard the group broadly, as the origin of the present much divided Liberal party that has, from the beginning of definite party organization, included a considerable numerical majority of the Cuban voters. In the first national election, held December 31, 1901, this group, the military group, appeared as the National party, supporting Tomas Estrada y Palma as its candidate. Its opponent was called the Republican party. Realizing its overwhelming defeat, the latter withdrew on the day of the election, alleging all manner of fraud and unfairness on the part of the Nationals. It is useless to follow in detail the history of Cuba's political parties since that time. In the election of 1905, the former National party appeared as the Liberal party, supporting José Miguel Gomez, while its opponents appeared as the Moderate party, supporting Estrada Palma who, first elected on what he declared to be a non-partisan basis, had definitely affiliated himself with the so-called Moderates. The election was a game of political crookedness on both sides, and the Liberals withdrew on election day. The result was the revolution of 1906. The Liberals split into factions, not yet harmonized, and the Moderate party became the Conservative party. By the fusion of some of the Liberal groups, that party carried the election of 1908, held under American auspices. A renewal of internal disorders, a quarrel among leaders, and much discontent with their administrative methods, resulted in the defeat of the Liberals in the campaign of 1912 and in the election of General Mario Menocal, the head of the Conservative ticket, and the present incumbent.

A fair presentation of political conditions in Cuba is exceedingly difficult, or rather it is difficult so to present them that they will be fairly understood. I have always regarded the establishment of the Cuban Republic in 1902 as premature, though probably unavoidable. A few years of experience with an autonomous government under American auspices, civil and not military, as a prologue to full independence, might have been the wiser course, but such a plan seemed impossible. The Cubans in the field had forced from Spain concessions that were satisfactory to many. Whether they could have forced more than that, without the physical assistance given by the United States, is perhaps doubtful. The matter might have been determined by the grant of the belligerent rights for which they repeatedly appealed to the United States. At no time in the entire experience did they ask for intervention. That came as the result of a combination of American wrath and American sympathy, and more in the interest of the United States than because of concern for the Cubans. But, their victory won and Spain expelled, the triumphant Cubans naturally desired immediate enjoyment of the fruits of victory. They desired to exercise the independence for which they had fought. Many protests and not a few threats of trouble attended even the brief period of American occupation. There was, moreover, an acute political issue in the United States. The peace and order declared as the purpose of American intervention had been established. The amendment to the Joint Resolution of April 20, 1898, disclaimed "any disposition or intention to exercise sovereignty, jurisdiction, or control over said Island except for the pacification thereof," etc. The island was pacified. The amendment asserted, further, the determination of the United States, pacification having been accomplished, "to leave the government and control of the island to its people." There was no pledge of any prolonged course of education in principles and methods of self-government. Nor did such education play any appreciable part in the experience of the American military government. The work of the interventors had been done in accordance with the specifications, and the Cubans were increasingly restless under a control that many of them, with no little reason, declared to be as autocratic as any ever exercised by Spain. Transfer and departure seemed to be the politic if not the only course, and we transferred and departed.

That these people, entirely without experience or training in self-government, should make mistakes was quite as inevitable as it is that a child in learning to walk will tumble down and bump its little nose. In addition to the inevitable mistakes, there have been occasional instances of deplorable misconduct on the part of individuals and of political parties. For neither mistakes nor misconduct can we criticize or condemn them without a similar criticism or condemnation of various experiences in our own history. We should, at least, regard them with charity. There are, moreover, incidents in the two experiences of American control of the island that, at least, border on the unwise and the discreditable. The only issue yet developed in Cuba is between good government and bad politics. The first President started admirably along the line of the former, and ended in a wretched tangle of the latter, though not at all by his own choice or direction. Official pre-eminence and a "government job" make quite the same appeal to the Cubans that they do to many thousands of Americans. So do raids on the national treasury, and profitable concessions. We see these motes in Cuban eyes somewhat more clearly than we see the beams in our own eyes. A necessarily slow process of political education is going on among the people, but in the meantime the situation has afforded opportunity for exploitation by an assortment of self-constituted political leaders who have adopted politics as a profession and a means of livelihood. Cuba's gravest danger lies in the political domination of men in this class. The present President, General Mario Menocal, is not in that group. The office sought him; he did not seek the office. Some of these self-constituted leaders have displayed a notable aptitude for political organization, and it is largely by means of the many little local organizations that the Cuban political game is played. Although, I believe, somewhat less now than formerly, the little groups follow and support individual leaders rather than parties or principles. Parties and their minor divisions are known by the names of their leaders. Thus, while both men are nominally of the same party, the Liberal, the adherents of José Miguel Gomez, are known as Miguelistas, and the adherents of Alfredo Zayas are known as Zayistas. Were either to announce himself as a Conservative, or to start a new party and call it Reformist or Progressive or any other title, he could count on being followed by most of those who supported him as a Liberal. This is a condition that will, in time, correct itself. What the Cuban really wants is what all people want, an orderly, honest, and economical government, under which he may live in peace and quiet, enjoying the fruits of his labor without paying an undue share of the fruits to maintain his government. For that the Cuban people took up arms against Spain. For a time they may be blinded by the idea of mere political independence, but to that same issue they will yet return by the route of the ballot-box. The game of politics for individual preferment, or for personal profit, cannot long be successfully played in Cuba, if I have rightly interpreted Cuban character and Cuban characteristics.

"We, the delegates of the people of Cuba, having met in constitutional convention for the purpose of preparing and adopting the fundamental law of their organization as an independent and sovereign people, establishing a government capable of fulfilling its international obligations, maintaining public peace, ensuring liberty, justice, and promoting the general welfare, do hereby agree upon and adopt the following constitution, invoking the protection of the Almighty. Article I. The people of Cuba are hereby constituted a sovereign and independent State and adopt a republican form of government." Thus opens the Constitution of the Republic of Cuba.

I recall an intensely dramatic moment connected with the closing phrase of the preamble. I have used a translation published by a distinguished Cuban. That phrase, in the original, is "*invocando el favor de Dios*," perhaps more exactly translated as "invoking the favor (or blessing) of God." When the Constitution had been drafted and broadly approved, it was submitted to the convention for suggestion of minor changes in verbiage. One of the oldest and most distinguished members of the body proposed that this phrase be left out. Another member, distinguished for his power as an orator and for his cynicism, in a speech of considerable length set forth his opinion that it made little difference whether it was included or excluded. There was no benefit in its inclusion, and no advantage in excluding it. It would hurt none and might please some to have it left in. Immediately across the semi-circle of desks, and facing these two speakers, sat Señor Pedro Llorente, a man of small stature, long, snow-white hair and beard, and a nervous and alert manner. At times, his nervous energy made him almost grotesque. At times, his absorbed earnestness made him, despite his stature, a figure of commanding dignity. Through the preceding addresses he waited with evident impatience. Obtaining recognition from the chairman, he rose and stood with upraised hand his voice tremulous with emotion, to protest against the proposed measure, declaring "as one not far from the close of life, that the body there assembled did not represent an atheistic people." The motion to strike out was lost, and the invocation remains.

The result of the deliberations of the Constitutional Convention is a highly creditable instrument. It contains a well-devised Bill of Rights, and makes all necessary provision for governmental organization and conduct. One feature, however, seems open to criticism. In their desire to avoid that form of centralized control, of which they had somewhat too much under Spanish power, the new institution provides, perhaps, for too much local government, for a too extensive provincial and municipal system. It has already fallen down in some respects, and it has become necessary to centralize certain functions, quite as it has become desirable in several of our own matters. Cuba has, perhaps, an undue overload of officialdom, somewhat too many public officers, and quite too many people on its pay-rolls. The feature of Cuba's Constitution that is of greatest interest and importance to the United States is what is known as the Platt Amendment. The provision for a Constitutional Convention in Cuba was made in what was known as Civil Order No. 301, issued by the Military Governor, on July 25, 1900. It provided for an election of delegates to meet in

Havana on the first Monday in November, following. The convention was to frame and adopt a Constitution and "as a part thereof, to provide for and agree with the Government of the United States upon the relations to exist between that Government and the Government of Cuba," etc. Against this, the Cubans protested vigorously. The United States had declared that "Cuba is and of right ought to be free and independent." The Cubans held, very properly, that definition of international relations had no fitting place in a Constitution "as a part thereof." Their point was recognized and, under date of November 5, Civil Order No. 310 was modified by Civil Order No. 455. That was issued to the delegates at the time of their assembly. It declared as follows: "It will be your duty, first, to frame and adopt a Constitution for Cuba, and, when that has been done, to formulate what, in your opinion, ought to be the relations between Cuba and the United States." Taking this as their programme, the delegates proceeded to draft a Constitution, leaving the matter of "relations" in abeyance for consideration at the proper time. Yet, before its work was done, the Convention was savagely criticized in the United States for its failure to include in the Constitution what it had been authorized, and virtually instructed, to leave out. The Constitution was completed on February 11, 1901, and was duly signed by the delegates, on February 21. A committee was appointed, on February 11, to prepare and submit plans and proposals regarding the matter of "relations." Prior to that, however, the matter had been frequently but informally discussed by the delegates. Suggestions had been made in the local press, and individual members of the Convention had expressed their views with considerable freedom. Had the United States kept its hands off at that time, a serious and critical situation, as well as a sense of injustice that has not yet entirely died out, would have been averted.

Before the Cubans had time to put their "opinion of what ought to be the relations" between the two countries into definite form, there was presented to them, in a manner as needless as it was tactless, a statement of what the American authorities thought those relations should be. The Cubans, who were faithfully observing their earlier instructions, were deeply offended by this interference, and by the way in which the interference came. The measures known as the Platt Amendment was submitted to the United States Senate, as an amendment to the Army Appropriation bill, on February 25, 1901 The Senate passed the bill, and the House concurred A storm of indignant protest swept over the island The Cubans believed, and not without reason, that the instrument abridged the independence of which they had been assured by those who now sought to limit that independence. Public opinion in the United States was divided. Some approved and some denounced the proceeding in bitter terms. The division was not at all on party lines. The situation in Cuba was entirely changed. Instead of formulating an opinion in accordance with their earlier instructions, the members of the Convention were confronted by a choice of what they then regarded as evils, acceptance of unacceptable terms or an indefinite continuance of a military government then no less unacceptable. A commission was sent to Washington to urge changes and modifications. It was given dinners, lunches, and receptions, but nothing more. At last the Cubans shrugged their shoulders. The desire for an immediate withdrawal of American authority, and for Cuban assumption of the reins of government, outweighed the objection to the terms imposed. A Cuban leader said: "There is no use in objecting to the inevitable. It is either annexation or a Republic with the Amendment. I prefer the latter." After four months of stubborn opposition, the Cubans yielded, by a vote of sixteen to eleven, with four absentees.

In many ways, the Cuban Government is like our own. The President and Vice-President are elected, through an electoral college, for a term of four years. A "third term" is specifically prohibited by the Constitution. Senators, four from each Province, are chosen, for a term of eight years, by an electoral board. Elections for one half of the body occur every four years. The House is chosen, by direct vote, for terms of four years, one half being elected every two years. The Cabinet, selected and appointed by the President, consists of eight Secretaries of Departments as follows: Agriculture, Commerce, and Labor; State; Government; Treasury (*Hacienda*); Public Instruction; Justice; Public Works; and Health and Charities. There is a Supreme Court, and there are the usual minor courts. The Constitution also makes provision for the organization and the powers of the Provincial and Municipal Governments. To the Constitution, the Platt Amendment is attached as an appendix, by treaty arrangement. As far as governmental system is concerned, Cuba is fairly well equipped; a possible source of danger is its over-equipment. Its laws permit, rather than require, an overburden of officials, high and low. But Cuba's governmental problem is essentially one of administration. Its particular obstacle in that department is professional politics.

The whole situation in Cuba is somewhat peculiar. The business of the island, that is, the commercial business, the purchase and sale of merchandise wholesale and retail, is almost entirely in the hands of Spaniards. The Cuban youths seldom become clerks in stores. Most of the so-called "*dependientes*" come out as boys from Spain. It is an old established system. These lads, almost invariably hard workers, usually eat and sleep in the place of their employment. The wage is small but board and lodging, such as the latter is, are furnished. They are well fed, and the whole system is quite paternal. For their recreation, education, and care in case of illness, there are organizations, half club and half mutual protective association, to which practically all belong. The fee is small and the benefits many. Some of these are based on a regional plan, that is, the *Centro de Asturianos* is composed of those who come from the Spanish province of Asturia, and those from other regions have their societies. There is also a general society of "*dependientes*." Some of these groups are rich, with large membership including not only the clerks of today but those of the last thirty or forty years, men who by diligence and thrift have risen to the top in Cuba's commercial life. Most of Cuba's business men continue their membership in these organizations, and many contribute liberally toward their maintenance.

This system more or less effectively bars Cuban youths from commercial life. Nor does commercial life seem attractive to more than a very limited number. This leaves to them, practically, only three lines of possible activity, the ownership and operation of a plantation, a profession, or manual labor. The greater number there, as elsewhere, are laborers, either on some little bit of ground they call their own or rent from its owner, or they are employed by the proprietors of the larger estates. Such proprietorship is, of course, open to only a few. The problem, which is both social and political, appears in a class that cannot or will not engage in manual labor, the well-educated or fairly-educated sons of men of fair income and a social position. Many of these take some professional course. But there is not room for so many in so small a country, and the professions are greatly overcrowded. The surplus either loafs and lives by its wits or at the expense of the family, or turns to the Government for a "job." It constitutes a considerable element on which the aspiring professional politician can draw for support. Having such "jobs," it constitutes a heavy burden on the tax-payers; deprived of its places on the Government pay-roll, it becomes a social and political menace. If a Liberal administration throws them out of their comfortable posts, they become noisy and perhaps violent Conservatives; if discharged by an economical Conservative administration, they become no less noisy and no less potentially violent Liberals. But we may not criticize. The American control that followed the insurrection of 1906 set no example in administrative economy for the Cubans to follow.

The productive industries of the island have already been reviewed in other chapters. The development of Cuba's commerce since the withdrawal of Spain, and the substitution of a modern fiscal policy for an antiquated and indefensible system, has been notable. It is, however, a mistake to contrast the present condition with the condition existing at the time of the American occupation, in 1899. The exact accuracy of the record is questionable, but the returns for the year 1894, the year preceding the revolution, show the total imports of the island as $77,000,000, and the total exports as $99,000,000. The probability is that a proper valuation would show a considerable advance in the value of the imports. The statement of export values may be accepted. It may be assumed that had there been no disorder, the trade of the island, by natural growth, would have reached $90,000,000 for imports and $120,000,000, for exports, in 1900. That may be regarded as a fair normal. As it was, the imports of that year were $72,000,000, and the exports, by reason of the general wreck of the sugar business, were only $45,000,000. With peace and order fairly assured, recovery came quickly. The exports of 1905, at $99,000,000, equalled those of 1894, while the imports materially exceeded those of the earlier year. In 1913, the exports reached $165,207,000, and the imports $132,290,000. This growth of Cuba's commerce and industry is due mainly to the economic requirements of the American people. We need Cuba's sugar and we want its tobacco. These two commodities represent about 90 per cent, of the total exports of the island. We buy nearly all of its sugar, under normal conditions, and about 60 per cent, of its tobacco and cigars. On the basis of the total commerce of the island, the records of recent years show this country as the source of supply for about 53 per cent, of Cuba's total imports, and as the market for about 83 per cent, of its exports.

A comparison of the years 1903 and 1913 shows a gain of about $87,000,000 in Cuba's total exports. Of this, about $75,000,000 is represented by sugar. The crop of 1894 a little exceeded a million tons. Such a quantity was not again produced until 1903. With yearly variations, due to weather conditions, later years show an enormous and unprecedented increase. The crops of 1913 and 1914 were, approximately, 2,500,000 tons each. The tobacco industry shows only a modest gain. The average value of the exports of that commodity has risen, in ten years, from about $25,000,000 to about $30,000,000. The increase in the industry appears largely in the shipment of leaf tobacco. The cigar business shows practically no change, in that time, as far as values are concerned. This résumé affords a fair idea of Cuba's trade expansion under the conditions established through the change in government. That event opened new and larger doors of opportunity, and the Cubans and others have been prompt in taking advantage of them. Toward the great increase shown, two forces have operated effectively. One is the treaty by which the provisions of the so-called Platt Amendment to the Cuban Constitution are made permanently effective. The other is the reciprocity treaty of 1903.

By the operation of the former of these instruments the United States virtually underwrites the political stability and the financial responsibility of the Cuban Government. That Government cannot borrow any important sums without the consent of the United States, and it has agreed that this country "may exercise the right to intervene for the preservation of Cuban independence, the maintenance of a government adequate for the protection of life, property, and individual liberty, and for discharging the obligations with respect to Cuba imposed by the Treaty of Paris on the United States." This assumption of responsibility by the United States inspired confidence on the part of capital, and large sums have been invested in Cuban bonds, and in numerous public and private enterprises. Railways and trolley lines have been built and many other works of public utility have been undertaken. The activities of old sugar plantations have been extended under improved conditions, and many new estates with costly modern equipment have been created. The cultivation of large areas, previously lying waste and idle, afforded both directly and indirectly employment for an increased population, as did the numerous public works. The other force, perhaps no less effective, appears in the reciprocity treaty of 1903. This gave to Cuba's most important crop a large though by no means absolute control of the constantly increasing sugar market of the United States, as far as competition from other foreign countries was concerned. The sugar industry of the island may be said to have been restored to its normal proportions in 1903. Our imports for the five-year period 1904-1908 averaged 1,200,000 tons a year. For the five-year period 1910-1914 they averaged 1,720,000 tons. In 1914, they were 2,200,000 tons as compared with 1,260,000 tons in 1904. It is doubtful if the treaty had any appreciable influence on the exports of Cuban tobacco to this country. We buy Cuba's special tobacco irrespective of a custom-house advantage that affects the box price only a little, and the price of a single cigar probably not at all. On the other side of the account, that of our sales to Cuba, there also appears a large increase since the application of the reciprocity treaty. Using the figures showing exports from the United States to Cuba, instead of Cuba's records showing imports from this country, it appears that our sales to the island in the fiscal year 1903, immediately preceding the operation of the treaty, amounted to $21,761,638. In the fiscal year 1913 they were $70,581,000, and in 1914 were $68,884,000.

Not all of this quite remarkable gain may properly be credited to the influence of the reciprocity treaty. The purchases of the island are determined, broadly, by its sales. As the latter increase, so do the former. Almost invariably, a year of large export sales is followed by a year of heavy import purchases. The fact that our imports from Cuba are double our sales to Cuba, in the total of a period of years, has given rise to some foolish criticism of the Cubans on the ground that, we buying so heavily from them, they should purchase from us a much larger percentage of their import requirements. No such obligation is held to exist in regard to our trade with other lands, and it should have no place in any consideration of our trade with Cuba. There are many markets, like Brazil, British India, Japan, China, Mexico, and Egypt, in which our purchases exceed our sales. There are more, like the United Kingdom, France, Germany, Italy, Canada, Central America, and numerous others, in which our sales considerably or greatly exceed our purchases. We do not buy from them simply because they buy from us. We buy what we need or want in that market in which we can buy to the greatest advantage. The Cuban merchants, who are nearly all Spaniards, do the same. The notion held by some that, because of our service to Cuba in the time of her struggle for national life, the Cubans should buy from us is both foolish and altogether unworthy. Any notion of Cuba's obligation to pay us for what we may have done for her should be promptly dismissed and forgotten. There are commodities, such as lumber, pork products, coal, wheat flour, and mineral oil produces, that Cuba can buy in our markets on terms better than those obtainable elsewhere. Other commodities, such as textiles, leather goods, sugar mill equipment, railway equipment, drugs, chemicals, and much else, must be sold by American dealers in sharp competition with the merchants of other countries, with such assistance as may be afforded by the reciprocity treaty. That instrument gives us a custom-house advantage of 20, 25, 30, and 40 per cent, in the tariff rates. It is enough in some cases to give us a fair equality with European sellers, and in a few cases to give us a narrow margin of advantage over them. It does not give us enough to compel Cuban buyers to trade with us because of lower delivered prices.

Cuba's economic future can be safely predicted on the basis of its past. The pace of its development will depend mainly upon a further influx of capital and an increase in its working population. Its political future is less certain. There is ample ground for both hope and belief that the little clouds that hang on the political horizon will be dissipated, that there will come, year by year, a sane adjustment to the new institutions. But full assurance of peace and order will come only when the people of the island, whether planters or peasants, see clearly the difference between a government conducted in their interest and a government conducted by Cubans along Spanish lines.

Echo Library
www.echo-library.com

Echo Library uses advanced digital print-on-demand technology to build and preserve an exciting world class collection of rare and out-of-print books, making them readily available for everyone to enjoy.

Situated just yards from Teddington Lock on the River Thames, Echo Library was founded in 2005 by Tom Cherrington, a specialist dealer in rare and antiquarian books with a passion for literature.

Please visit our website for a complete catalogue of our books, which includes foreign language titles.

The Right to Read
Echo Library actively supports the Royal National Institute of the Blind's Right to Read initiative by publishing a comprehensive range of large print and clear print titles.

Large Print titles are in 16 point Tiresias font as recommended by the RNIB.

Clear Print titles are in 13 point Tiresias font and designed for those who find standard print difficult to read.

Customer Service
If there is a serious error in the text or layout please send details to feedback@echo-library.com and we will supply a corrected copy. If there is a printing fault or the book is damaged please refer to your supplier.

Printed in the United States
127577LV00002BA/12/A